Muslim and Jew

T0316338

Muslim and Jew: Origins, Growth, Resentment seeks to show how and why Islam and Judaism have been involved in political and theological self-definitions using the other since the seventh century. This short volume provides a historical and comparative survey of how each religion has thought about the other and, in so doing, about itself. It confines itself to those points at which Judaism and Islam intersect and cross-pollinate, and explores how this delicate process continues into the present with the Israeli–Palestinian conflict.

Muslim and Jew thus seeks to move beyond the intersection of a monolithic Judaism and a monolithic Islam and instead examines and organizes the messiness of the encounter as both religions sought to define themselves within, from, and against the other.

Aaron W. Hughes is the Philip S. Bernstein Professor in the Department of Religion and Classics at the University of Rochester. His numerous books include *Abrahamic Religions: On the Uses and Abuses of History* (2012), *Muslim Identities: An Introduction to Islam* (2013), and *Shared Identities: Medieval and Modern Imaginings of Judeo-Islam* (2017).

Routledge Focus on Religion

Amoris Laetitia and the spirit of Vatican II
The Source of Controversy
Mariusz Biliniewicz

Muslim and Jew
Origins, Growth, Resentment
Aaron W. Hughes

For more information about this series, please visit: www.routledge.com/ Routledge-Focus-on-Religion/book-series/RFR

Muslim and Jew

Origins, Growth, Resentment

Aaron W. Hughes

Routledge
Taylor & Francis Group

LONDON AND NEW YORK

First published 2019 by Routledge

2 Park Square, Milton Park, Abingdon, Oxfordshire OX14 4RN

52 Vanderbilt Avenue, New York, NY 10017

Routledge is an imprint of the Taylor & Francis Group, an informa business

First issued in paperback 2020

British Library Cataloguing-in-Publication Data
A catalogue record for this book is available from the British Library

Library of Congress Cataloging-in-Publication Data
Names: Hughes, Aaron W., 1968– author.
Title: Muslim and Jew : origins, growth, resentment / Aaron W. Hughes.
Description: 1 [edition]. | New York : Routledge, 2018. | Series: Routledge
   focus on religion | Includes bibliographical references and index.
Identifiers: LCCN 2018040834 | ISBN 9781138599444 (hardback) |
   ISBN 9780429023828 (ebook)
Subjects: LCSH: Judaism—Relations—Islam. | Islam—Relations—Judaism.
Classification: LCC BP173.J8 H835 2018 | DDC 296.3/9—dc23
LC record available at https://lccn.loc.gov/2018040834

ISBN: 978-1-138-59944-4 (hbk)
ISBN: 978-0-367-60662-6 (pbk)

Typeset in Times New Roman
by Apex CoVantage, LLC

a liliana
"Un solo istante i palpiti del suo bel cor sentir!"

Contents

Preface

The phrase "Muslim and Jew" unfortunately conjures up a series of unsavory images that revolve around military occupation and violent resistance in the modern Middle East. At risk of being subsumed in the midst of such violence is the fact that these two peoples, including their religions, have been in close contact with one another for close to fifteen hundred years. They have lived beside one another, they have thought with one another, and they have defined themselves using the other's literal and metaphorical language. Changes in one religion, moreover, have inevitably created repercussions in the other. These encounters, whether benign or bellicose, generate a set of anxieties as each seeks to better depict and delineate itself. The result is that each group desires to carve out space – be it social, intellectual, religious, economic, cultural, and now increasingly geographic – for itself in the light of its proximity to the other. The present is not unique, then, but merely one iteration of a long and complex relationship.

Those who work on the Israeli-Palestinian conflict, however, tend not to connect the current impasse to the medieval period, let alone to the time of Islamic origins in the seventh century. Instead, they prefer to locate the motive for conflict with the rise of Zionism in the 1880s and the subsequent Arab resistance to it. While I certainly do not fault them for this tendency, it all too quickly overlooks the lengthy period prior to that wherein Jews and Muslims interacted. The anxiety produced by the contemporary Israeli-Palestinian conflict, I wish to suggest in the pages that follow, is structurally similar to that produced by earlier iterations of Muslim-Jewish cohabitation. Proximity and the concomitant need for differentiation create a set of conditions that can produce creativity and conflict, often simultaneously. The present study uses a much larger canvas than is traditionally utilized in order to see if we can learn anything about the present conflict from previous encounters. I certainly would not want to imply that there is some deep-seated conflict between Jew and Muslim or even that the convoluted history between these two social groups inevitably has to culminate in the antagonism and violence to which we are increasingly habituated. Instead, I maintain that the past – especially when denuded of romanticism or finger-pointing – can actually help us to illumine aspects of the present. Jews and Muslims, not unlike Israelis and Palestinians, have been caught up in a dialectic of self-definition and other-abnegation since their first encounter with one another.

In the early 1950s, Shlomo Dov Goitein put pen to paper and began what would go on to be a short and masterful history of the relationship between Jews and Muslims titled *Jews and Arabs: Their Contacts Through the Ages.*[1] Perhaps not coincidentally, he wrote this work just after the formation of the State of Israel in 1948 and at a time when Yemenite Jews – to whom he referred as "the most genuine Jews living amongst the most genuine Arabs" – were about to be resettled in the newly formed country.[2] Their socioeconomic isolation and physical separation "from the body of the nation" meant, for Goitein, that the Jews of Yemen embodied in both their customs and their traditions an authentic form of Judaism, one that had been hidden by more cosmopolitan forms.[3] Their subsequent repatriation to Israel thus symbolized the return of the entire Jewish people to their primordial and subterranean origins.

Goitein sought to understand these Yemeni Jews in their social, linguistic, and historical contexts. However, it is also clear that his own situatedness played a not insignificant role in how he imagined both "Jew" and "Muslim." His exposition – in equal parts romantic, Orientalist, and essentialist – was based on problematic assertions of "authenticity," and he imagined Jews and Arabs as "cousins" who shared a set of common traits that "can best be described as those of a *primitive democracy*."[4] Goitein further argued that it was this political orientation that differentiated them from the great civilizations that surrounded them. "Against the background of the civilization of the ancient Orient," he continues,

> Israel and the Arabs present the type of a society which is characterized by the absence of privileged castes and classes, by the absence of enforced obedience to a strong authority, by undefined but nonetheless very powerful agencies for the formation and expression of

public opinion, by freedom of speech, and by a high respect for human life, dignity and freedom.[5]

Goitein coined the term "symbiosis" to refer to this intimate relationship between Jews and Arabs. It is a term that has been used consistently ever since. At its most basic level, the narrative that this metaphor structures goes something like the following: Judaism helped to give birth to Islam in the late sixth century on the Arabian Peninsula before Islam returned the favor in the tenth to twelfth centuries in places like Baghdad and Muslim Spain by facilitating the rise and florescence of, among other things, Hebrew belles-lettres and Jewish theology. Symbiosis seems to have allowed Goitein, as indeed it does to those who have followed in his footsteps,[6] a way to maintain Jewish difference within a dominant Muslim culture all the while still affording Jews with the opportunity to be full participants within it.[7]

Goitein goes even further, however, and subsequently taxonomizes symbiosis into four discrete stages. The first, the "pre-historical," stretches from the period of common origins to roughly 500 CE. This period, according to him, was marked by "common social patterns" derived from their shared "primitive democracy." The second phase, that of "creative Jewish–Arab symbiosis," lasted from roughly the time of the origins of Islam in the late sixth century CE to around 1300, the end of which he calls the high Middle Ages. The third stretched from 1300 to 1900, when, for him, the Arabs "faded out" from world history. The fourth is the twentieth century, a period of increased and growing confrontation between the two peoples. In this period, "the Westernized Jewish people is again connected with the original scene of its history, the Orient, while the Arab, although revived under Western impact and with Western help, still are inclined to oppose the West and with it Israel as its closest representative."[8]

Goitein's work would undergo several editions over the years, and, to this day, the volume remains an impressive, if increasingly problematic, account. Despite more recent editions, we cannot deny that it remains more than 60 years old, and recycles many assumptions about religion and about ethnic identity that betray an earlier generation of scholarship. Goitein's use of discrete religions (Judaism and Islam) that automatically and necessarily predetermine how individuals (Jew and Muslim) think or structure the world, his implication of their religions' unchangeable or immutable essences, and his characterization of fluid social groups as if they were stable all need to be revisited and, in the process, systematically rethought.

The slim volume that follows presents, for lack of a better term, a "post-symbiotic" treatment of Jewish-Muslim relations. It works on the assumption that, ever since their first encounter, Jews and Muslims have defined themselves with the other. There was then no monolithic "Judaism," in other words, that interacted with some monolithic "Islam." Instead there were various groups who shared a similar vocabulary and often overlapping intellectual or religious concerns (e.g., apocalypticism, belief in one God) and who increasingly defined themselves by what they were not. The account that follows, thus, seeks to avoid the interaction of discrete religions that has been such a common byproduct of the secondary literature. Instead it focuses on social groups who appealed to religions, often in retrospect, and this concomitantly shows the messiness of social interactions and, in the process, of self-definition. In so doing, it seeks to dislodge the basic narrative that "symbiosis" tells by avoiding appeals to well-defined and stable essences, whether of the Jewish or the Muslim variety. My aim, then, is to show how and why these two religious traditions have been involved in the constant need for self-definition and self-calibration, often in ways that use and abuse the other, since roughly the beginning of the seventh century.

It is not a story in which the present situation should be regarded as incongruous with the past, however. Nor is it a story in which the two groups and their religions are fundamentally incompatible with one another. Far from it, the past replays – albeit with a greater concern for a physical boundary and with a predominantly secular overlay – a set of issues that should be familiar to anyone with an understanding of the past relationship between these two religions.

Notes

1 It would undergo subsequent editions in 1964, 1970, and 1974, and in 2005 would be reissued with a new subtitle: "A Concise History of Their Social and Cultural Relations."
2 Shlomo Dov Goitein, *Jews and Arabs: Their Contacts Through the Ages* (New York: Schocken, 1955), vii.
3 Shlomo Dov Goitein, *The Yemenites: History, Social Orders, Spiritual Life*, ed. Menachem Ben-Sasson (Jerusalem: Yad Ben-Zvi and the Hebrew University of Jerusalem, 1983), 241.
4 Goitein, *Jews and Arabs*, 27.
5 Goitein, *Jews and Arabs*, 27.

6 More recent examples include Bernard Lewis, *The Jews of Islam* (Princeton: Princeton University Press, 78); Sarah Stroumsa, *Maimonides in His World: Portrait of a Mediterranean Thinker* (Princeton: Princeton University Press, 2009), 5.
7 I provide a full-scale rethinking of this metaphor, and all that it structures, in my *Shared Identities: Medieval and Modern Imaginings of Judeo-Islam* (New York: Oxford University Press, 2017), 17–35.
8 Goitein, *Jews and Arabs*, 11.

Acknowledgments

I would like to thank Rebecca Shillabeer, my editor at Routledge. In 2017, I published a technical volume: *Shared Identities: Medieval and Modern Imaginings of Judeo-Islam*. To quote myself therein, "what was supposed to be a nontechnical introduction meant primarily for an undergraduate and interested lay readership began to transform into a study of language and ultimately one of comparison" (xi). At that point I did not have the vocabulary to write a readable and accessible narrative of Jewish-Muslim relations that would avoid falling back on a wistful and romantic reading of the past. I thus used Rebecca's kind invitation to write a short history of Jewish and Muslim relations for *Routledge Focus* as a way to imagine a more accessible introduction of that earlier volume for what I hope will be a more general reading audience. I would also like to thank the two anonymous readers for the press, who helped me to tighten up my argument in several places.

I have been fortunate to have many interlocutors for my larger project of rewriting the story of Jewish-Muslim relations. Parts of the argument found herein have been presented at Yale University, Emory University, Aga Khan University in London, Freie Universität of Berlin, University of Freiburg, the Belgian Academy in Rome, Otago University in New Zealand, and the Nangeroni Seminar on Islamic Origins in Florence. I would like to thank my hosts and conversation partners in all of those locations: Liran Yadgar, Frank Griffel, Eric L. Goldstein, Philip Wood, Leif Stenberg, Manolis Ulbrecht, Adam Walker, Majid Daneshgar, Johanna Pink, Simon Wolfgang Fuchs, Ghazzal Dabiri, Will Sweetman, Ben Schonthal, John Shaver, Tommaso Tesei, and Guillaume Dye.

In addition to the aforementioned I would like to thank the usual cast of characters, with whom I regularly talk and have been doing so moreover for most of my career: the late Kalman Bland, Willi Braun, Russell McCutcheon, James T. Robinson, Elliot R. Wolfson, and Donald Wiebe.

Chapter One had its origin in "Religion Without Religion: Integrating Islamic Origins into Religious Studies," *Journal of the American Academy of Religion* 85.4 (2017): 867–888. Chapter Two reworks, albeit with a new argument and concern, two chapters ("Theology: The Articulation of Orthodoxy" and "Mysticism: The Quest for Transcendence"), both of which appeared in *The Routledge Handbook of Muslim-Jewish Relations*, ed. Josef Meri (London and New York: Routledge, 2016), 77–94 and 219–234 respectively. Chapter Three, in addition to the main frame of the entire narrative, is new.

A word on transliteration

Since this is meant as an introduction to a complex relationship meant for a general readership, I have opted not to place diacritics on Arabic and Hebrew names and terms. I have, however, left them on bibliographic citations, when they appear in the original.

Introduction

The anatomy of a relationship

In the Spring of 2018 groups of Palestinian Arabs in the Gaza Strip decided to protest their untenable living conditions, exacerbated by the extended Israeli blockade, and marched to the border with Israel. While most demonstrated peacefully, groups of young men approached the border with burning tires and began throwing stones at Israeli troops. The latter accused Hamas of encouraging an invasion and responded by firing live ammunition into the protestors, killing more than 110 individuals and wounding thousands. These protests, certainly not coincidentally, coincided with the movement of the American Embassy in Israel from Tel Aviv to Jerusalem on May 14, which that year coincided for Israelis with *yom ha-atzmaut* ("Independence Day") and for Palestinians with *yawm al-nakhba* ("Day of Catastrophe").

This dialectic of independence for one group and catastrophe for the other reveals clearly the struggle, and indeed symbolizes the heavy price that has been paid, as two nationalist movements clash over one piece of land. How is it possible to find a durable peace between two peoples with radically different understandings of land, compromise, and victimhood? Amos Oz, an Israeli novelist and peace activist, proposes divorce as a solution. "Once divorced, let us experience coexistence and leave notions of possible cohabitation to future generations," he writes, for "ours is not a Hollywood western of good vs. evil. It is a real life tragedy of two just causes. We can continue to clash, inflicting further pain. Or we can be reconciled via separation and compromise."[1] Implicit in divorce is the memory of a shared life despite mutual recriminations, a collective journey of self-discovery if now ended, and the nostalgia for what might otherwise have been. Divorce between peoples is, after all, no less painful or difficult than it is among former spouses.

I like Oz's metaphor of divorce on account of its invocation of the intimacy of the relation between these two peoples. While I suggest something similar in the conclusion to this volume, it is necessary to realize that even divorce does not spell the end, but only a new and different beginning. Even the proposed "two-state solution" – wherein a State of Palestine takes up its place next to the State of Israel – implies a modus vivendi that, while it will imply a new chapter in their relationship, will not be novel or without precedents.

The Israeli-Palestinian conflict, as even the quickest glance at a newspaper or television screen will reveal, is ubiquitous if not omnipresent. We should not mistake it, however, for an eternal clash between two peoples based on biblical precedent, let alone for a clash of civilizations. It is instead but the latest installment in a much larger narrative of Jewish-Muslim relations, one that will certainly not be closed at any point in the near or even distant future. While the current installment happens to be defined by mistrust, bloodshed, and an unwillingness to engage in political compromise, it tells but one part of a meanderingly complex story between two interconnected groups. Despite the dire situation of the present, relations, including tensions, between them are certainly not new, but part of an ongoing process whereby Jews and Muslims have interacted with one another from the very beginning. Indeed, this interaction constantly revolves around the triangulated themes of encounter, anxiety, and self-definition (which, by definition, includes other-abnegation). These themes form the leitmotifs that link the disparate chapters that follow.

****

A not insignificant question is how does one tell the narrative of Jewish-Muslim relations? What metaphors, for example, does one choose to employ, and which individuals and events ought one to emphasize? Such choice is never value neutral and not infrequently determines the conclusions reached. There is, for instance, a danger of retelling this story using the prism of romantic wistfulness. This tends to be our default narrative and is based on the assumption that Jew and Muslim, erstwhile mutual descendants of Abraham, have so much in common and have gotten along for so much of their history that the present is but a blemish on what is imagined as an otherwise peaceful coexistence.[2] According to this narrative, if today's Jews and Muslims could only recognize their shared patrimony and history, things might get better once again.[3] We see this narrative invoked, for example, by politicians and even scholars who point to a "golden age" of coexistence in places such as the Iberian Peninsula in the tenth and eleventh centuries.

Coexisting alongside this romantic narrative is an equally problematic one. I call this the "lachrymose" approach. It views the exact same history of Jewish-Muslim relations but tends to do so through a significantly and often radically different prism. Rather than see coexistence, for example, those who adhere to this interpretive framework see persecution, destruction, and even anti-Semitism.[4] According to them, Islam has from its very beginnings been an intolerant tradition that, despite legal assurances to the contrary, has consistently made life arduous for religious minorities.

Needless to say both of these narratives, the romantic and the lachrymose, are based more on political expediency than on the historical record. Those who imagine an intolerant Islam in history, and they invariably tend to be of the right-of-center persuasion, try to score political points for their own bellicose viewpoint in the present. Those who imagine a tolerant Islam, to use the other narrative, seek to hold out a monotheistic lifeline to offer an ecumenical respite from the storms of our messy present.

The present analysis acknowledges the tidy portraits that these two narratives present, and seeks to avoid the extremes of romanticism on the one hand and fear-mongering on the other. Unlike the interests of these two narratives, my interest is not in providing a neat and tidy presentation that pivots around unnuanced propositions, such as "Islam is x" or the "genius of Judaism is y." Such essentialisms, the hallmark of an earlier generation of Orientalists and comparative religionists, prove unhelpful to an understanding of the historical record wherein groups or people rarely divide neatly, let alone solely, between discrete religions. While common in the media and in popular opinion, such essentialisms obscure rather than facilitate historical appreciation on many different levels. This present volume is less interested in such reifications and is instead interested in the messiness of the interactions between social groups who appeal to "Judaism" and/or "Islam" in specific historical and social contexts. Rather than envisage monolithic and timeless religious traditions – to wit, Islam and Judaism – interacting with and influencing one another in some essentialist vacuum, I prefer to imagine a more complicated process.

This takes the form, at the bare minimum, of at least two types of interaction. Initially, and in the beginning of their historical interactions, indiscrete social groups needed to distinguish themselves from those who appeared as too much like them. This, perhaps not surprisingly, led to various discourses of differentiation, in which Jews and Muslims defined themselves both by what they were (or hoped to be) and by what they were not. Later on, as boundaries between these groups began to solidify, more discrete groups began to use the other, whether real or imagined, to further define themselves on the one hand and distance themselves from the other. It is in these historical groups inhabiting distinct social contexts, in other words, and not simply disembodied religious traditions, that we witness the ways in which Jews and Muslims thought about one another and, in the process, thought about themselves and their own realities. Judaism and Islam, on this reading, are little more than categories or, perhaps better, literary topoi to which groups could and did appeal to make sense of themselves and the various worlds that they inhabited. The situation today, again as should be clear from even the quickest glance at a newspaper, has not radically changed.

****

Jews and Muslims, then, have interacted with one another ever since Muhammad began to preach his apocalyptic message of monotheism to fellow tribesmen at the beginning of the seventh century CE. What Islam and Judaism looked like on the Arabian Peninsula at this time, however, would certainly have been considerably different from the world religions that we today recognize. Centuries of coalescence and crystallization within and between the two religions – as embodied in, but surely not limited to, key individuals – would introduce numerous theological, liturgical, and doctrinal similarities between them. It is on this macro-level that we tend to posit similarities or differences between the two religions.[5] The problem, though, is that ever since the nineteenth century such similarities have largely been reduced to that of "influence."[6] This usually takes the following historical structure: in the beginning Judaism's ideas functioned as a midwife to the birth of Islam, not unlike how they had at Christianity's birth several centuries earlier, and this was subsequently reversed several centuries later in places like al-Andalus (Muslim Spain) when Islam gave Judaism a new literary and philosophical vocabulary in which to articulate itself. This grandiose narrative framework, however, abhors complexity and in its place prefers to situate discrete groups of Jews and Muslims that interact without ever incurring major transformations because the cores of each religion are imagined to exist beyond history.

In recent years scholars have begun to complicate the narrative of how Christianity and Judaism came to separate from one another.[7] This often means taking a less sanguine approach to our historical and literary sources. Rather than simply accept later sources as historical transcripts of what actually happened, scholars of late antiquity have instead begun to argue that we ought to situate these sources against a broader, and often much later, set of theological interests and political agendas. Instead of reading sources as offering unmediated access into what really transpired, then, such scholars posit a much messier social world wherein overlapping groups of Christians and Jews – not infrequently referred to as "Jewish-Christians" (or "Judaizing Christians") or "Christian-Jews" (or "Christianizing Jews") – sought to carve out epistemic space for themselves, and their teachings, in light of the investment in, and concomitant desire to separate from, the other.

Such a model is increasingly accepted as part of how we conceive of Jewish-Christian relations at the beginning of the late antique period. It may come as a surprise to learn, however, that many are content to assume that the situation at the other end of late antiquity, that is, at the advent of Islam, was much *less* complex. Rather than show the diversity of religious forms, many are content to work on the assumption that Judaism simply provided the raw materials from which Islam emerged and ultimately drew inspiration. Methodologically this returns us to a similar grid as noted earlier: later Muslim sources are taken at face value and as providing eyewitness accounts of what really happened. In these later sources the early Muslim community is described, for example, as encountering normative rabbinic Jews to whom Muhammad, at least initially, was favorably predisposed, before becoming increasingly disillusioned with their perfidy. There is a tendency, in other words, to use later rabbinic Jews whom subsequent framers of Islam would have encountered in cosmopolitan centers such as ninth-century Baghdad and whom they would then have retroactively projected back onto the time of Muhammad. The only problem with such a position, and it is often seen as beyond questioning, is that we do not possess a shred of evidence for any such claims to normativity.[8]

In like manner, our inherited narrative of Muslim-Jewish relations in the medieval period works on the assumption that Jews and Muslims interacted, that Jews absorbed the ideas of Muslims, and that they began to use these ideas to articulate Judaism. I wish to go a step further and argue that such Jewish intellectuals sought to create an "Islamic Judaism," one wherein Islam fundamentally altered the way in which Judaism would forever be conceived. They did not usher in a simple set of cosmetic changes. On the contrary, they fundamentally transformed Judaism. In like manner, I wish to suggest that Muslim theologians, much less cognizant of Judaism (as is the privilege of the majority), constructed Islamic orthodoxy by using the trope of "Jew" or "Judaism" to apply to Muslim groups (e.g., the Shia) that would later be labeled as heterodox.

This mutual self-definition was not confined to the medieval period. It continues, as the third part of the study will show, into the modern period.

Theology and the construction of the other

The prism through which I have chosen to frame my analysis is that of "theology." On account of the fact that this term is neither Jewish nor Muslim, its use certainly deserves scrutiny. The term derives from the Greek *theos* and *logia*, which, when combined, refers to those rational discourses created about God or the divine world. Those who undertake its activity are accordingly referred to as theologians. When transferred onto an English register, theology refers to the articulation of truth claims developed by a specific religion or religious tradition. This articulation can refer not only to metaphysical claims (e.g., God's attributes, freewill v. determinism), but also to ontological (e.g., what is a human?) and ethical ones (e.g., how does one relate to others, including those of different religious communities?). Theology, in other words, is the manner whereby a religious community thinks about itself, about others, and about how they should interact with one another on account of some divine agency, whether real or perceived. Theology, on my reading, becomes the script whereby a group situates itself, ideally and theoretically, within a social space. Theology, in what follows, is not about actual truth claims, but about how the construction of truth claims tells us how social groups imagine themselves and others. My interest then takes place on what we might call the level of social construction.[9]

Traditional theology is concerned with topics such as the nature of God, the relationship between God and humans, providence, the existence of evil, and the problem of freewill vis-à-vis determinism, to name but a few. My concern here, however, is much less philosophical. It is, as just mentioned, both with the discourses associated with treatment of *the* other (for Muslims, this would be Jews and vice versa) and with how and why such discourses emerged in the first place. These discourses reveal to us something of the processes – sociological, religious, intellectual, and cultural – with which each group thought about the other and, by this very act, about itself. This means that it is important, following the lead of Ross Brann, that we examine what he calls the "textual manifestations of Jewish and Muslim literary productions to get a sense of the anxieties that each group produced in the other."[10] In this, we might do well to invoke the words of Jonathan Z. Smith:

> While the "other" may be perceived as being either LIKE-US or NOT-LIKE-US, he is in fact, most problematic when he is TOO-MUCH-LIKE-US, or when he claims to BE-US. It is here that the real urgency of a "theory of the self" emerges. This urgency is called forth not by the requirement to place the "other," but rather to situate ourselves. . . . The problem is not alterity, but similarity – at times, even identity. A "theory of the other" is but another way of phrasing a "theory of the self."[11]

Smith here reminds us that because other groups who dwell in close proximity are often "too much like us" they need to be theorized and categorized in relation to us.

My argument in what follows is that, on account of their close proximity to one another, Jews and Muslims needed (and indeed continue to need) to construct narratives of the self that were in turn motivated by narratives of the other. This means that when each group writes about the other they are often less concerned about the actua other than they are about the self.

Breakdown of chapters

The book is divided into three distinct chapters, each of which refers to a particular time period. The first chapter, "Origins," examines the late antique period and argues that theology – though I doubt either group would have employed this term – was the primary means whereby Jews and Muslims differentiated themselves from one another after a period of fluidity on the Arabian Peninsula. Judaism, it is frequently assumed, is the stable entity that gives birth to a nascent Islam. Rarely broached, however, is just how little we actually know about these Jews of the Arabian Peninsula in the fifth and sixth centuries CE. On account of such taxonomical difficulties, it is impossible to witness a clearly defined break between the two religions, one wherein certain beliefs and practices would have been easily identifiable as "Jewish" or "Muslim." I instead argue that both Judaism and Islam emerged at the same time, and often in ways that were indistinct from one another.

The second chapter, "Growth," charts the relationship between Muslim and Jew in the medieval period. Now Jews developed theological principles that they learned from Muslim theologians (*mutakallimun*), especially those associated with the Mutazila school. I argue that after the rise of Islam and its political dominance in the region, Judaism was poorly or underdefined, with many groups exploring different paradigms of leadership and structures of authority. All of this was to change with the career of Saadya Gaon (882–942), who articulated a theological vocabulary that sought to define clearly what Judaism was or ought to be. In so doing, however, he adopted the literal (Arabic) and metaphorical (theological) language of Islam. This adoption, I suggest, facilitated the creation of an "Islamic Judaism." It is, moreover, an activity in which many subsequent Jewish thinkers would engage.

The third chapter, "Resentment," focuses on the modern period to examine the Israeli-Palestinian conflict as a window onto contemporary Jewish-Muslim relations. While I certainly realize that not all Muslims are Palestinians and not all Palestinians are Muslims, this conflict nonetheless provides a convenient lens to shine light on how each continues to think about itself by thinking about the other. The anxiety produced by the lack of a geographic border mimics the lack of social and religious borders from the previous two chapters. Though I will focus on the political conflict – and the chapter will, at times, read as one of political science – I need to do this in order to get at the larger point I wish to make, which returns us to the larger theme of the volume.

Notes

1 Amos Oz, "For Its Survival, Israel Must Abandon the One-State Option," *Los Angeles Times*, March 7, 2015.
2 On the problems of this narrative and for a survey of the uses to which it has been put, see my *Abrahamic Religions: On the Uses and Abuses of History* (New York and Oxford: Oxford University Press, 2012).
3 For egregious examples, see Karl-Josef Kuschel, *Abraham: Sign of Hope for Jews, Christians, and Muslims*, trans. John Dowden (New York: Continuum, 1995); María Rosa Menocal, *The Ornament of the World: How Muslims, Jews, and Christians Created a Culture of Tolerance in Medieval Spain* (New York: Back Bay Books, 2002); Chris Lowney, *A Vanished World:*

Muslims, Christians, and Jews in Medieval Spain (New York: Oxford University Press, 2005).

4 Egregious examples include Bat Yeor, *The Dhimmi: Jews & Christians Under Islam*, trans. David Maisel (Madison: Fairleigh Dickinson University Press, 1985); *The Myth of Islamic Tolerance: How Islamic Law Treats Non-Muslims*, ed. Robert Spencer (Amherst: Prometheus Books, 2005); Dario Fernandez-Morera, *The Myth of Andalusian Paradise: Muslims, Christians, and Jews Under Islamic Rule in Muslim Spain* (Wilmington: ISI Books, 2016).

5 See, e.g., *Judaism and Islam in Practice: A Sourcebook*, eds. Jacob Neusner, Tamara Sonn, and Jonathan E. Brockopp (London: Routledge, 2005).

6 On the problems engendered by this term and trope in history, see the criticisms of the so-called Cambridge school, which tries to avoid analyzing texts using the traditional model of influences/anticipations on account of its propensity toward anachronisms. See, in particular, Quentin Skinner, "Meaning and Understanding in the History of Ideas," *History and Theory* 8 (1969): 3–53; idem, *The Foundations of Modern Political Thought* (Cambridge: Cambridge University Press, 1978), x–xv.

7 See, e.g., Andrew S. Jacobs, *Christ Circumcised: A Study in Early Christian History and Difference* (Philadelphia: University of Pennsylvania Press, 2012); Natalie Dohrmann and Annette Yoshiko Reed, "Introduction," in *Jews, Christians, and the Roman Empire: The Poetics of Power in Late Antiquity*, eds. N. Dohrmann and A. Y. Reed (Philadelphia: University of Pennsylvania Press, 2013), 1–22; Daniel Boyarin, *Border Lines: The Partition of Judaeo-Christianity* (Philadelphia: University of Pennsylvania Press, 2014).

8 Two recent treatments, for example, reproduce this basic narrative. See Gordon D. Newby, *A History of the Jews of Arabia: From Ancient Times to Their Eclipse Under Early Islam* (Columbia: University of South Carolina Press, 1988); Haggai Mazuz, *The Religious and Spiritual Life of the Jews of Medina* (Leiden: Brill, 2014).

9 See, e.g., Jean-François Bayart, *The Illusion of Cultural Identity*, trans. Steven Rendell et al. (Chicago: University of Chicago Press, 2005); Richard Jenkins, *Rethinking Ethnicity* (London: Sage, 2008).

10 See, e.g., the sensitive treatment in Ross Brann, *Power in the Portrayal: Representations of Jews and Muslims in Eleventh- and Twelfth-Century Islamic Spain* (Princeton: Princeton University Press, 2002), 7–10.

11 Jonathan Z. Smith, "What a Difference a Difference Makes," in *"To See Ourselves as Others See Us": Christians, Jews, and "Others" in Late Antiquity*, eds. Jacob Neusner and Ernest Frerichs (Chico: Scholars Press, 1985), 3–49 at 47.

1 Origins

Standard histories of Jewish-Muslim relations tend to begin with the birth of Muhammad sometime around the year 570 CE and then proceed to recount his subsequent interactions with the Jews of the Arabian Peninsula.[1] Islam, according to this paradigm, is the product of a late antique environment in which existed other monotheisms that, in turn, must have played some sort of role in this new religion's emergence. Using the old to shine light on the new or the transparent to illumine the inchoate would certainly seem like the most obvious point of departure. There are, however, a number of historical, textual, and categorical problems with this framework that are frequently suppressed. Stated in the most basic terms and to be analyzed in more detail in what follows: we possess very little historical evidence for the rise of Islam; most of our sources describing its appearance date to later generations; and, especially relevant to this study, what constituted "Jewishness" and "Muslimness" at this time and in this particular locale is anything but clear.[2]

The major way to bypass such problems is to treat the later sources as transcripts of what actually happened. Though inaccurate, for many such an approach solves the problem of historicity and firms up the boundary between Jew and Muslim, and Judaism and Islam. This approach, however, generates more problems than answers since it ultimately produces little more than a portrait of what later generations wanted to happen as opposed to what really happened. According to later traditions, for example, the Jews with whom Muhammad interacted would have descended from those who escaped the destruction of the Second Temple in 70 CE. These Arabian Jews, it is further assumed, then functioned – along with other clearly defined religious groups in the area, such as Christians and Manicheans – as important resources for the birth of Muhammad's new message of monotheism. As we shall see in this chapter, however, it is not at all clear what groups who professed these religions actually believed, let alone practiced. We should also not rule out the possibility that later sources tended to imagine particular groups as "Jewish" when, in fact, they may well not have been. It seems unlikely, for example, that Arabian Jews were rabbinic, since rabbinic Judaism did not emerge until as late as the sixth century and probably much later in more peripheral areas.[3] What forms of Christianity existed on the Arabian Peninsula in the sixth century is equally unclear. Our dominant "world religions" paradigm that posits the discrete religions of later centuries and retroactively projects them back onto late antiquity thus proves to be unhelpful in reconstructing the events that transpired at the advent of Islam. Though the later paradigm has the advantage of providing a tidy picture, I hope it should be clear already that the historical record is much more complex. Moreover, since social groups interact with one another, and not disembodied religions, it becomes necessary to appreciate the messiness and the complexity of social interactions as opposed to assigning problematic terms such as "anticipations" or "influences."

In addition to such anachronisms, we would also do well to pay attention to the contemporary political undertones when it comes to dealing with Jewish-Muslim relations in these early years. This usually takes the form of assuming that Islam is not particularly original, but is instead the simple sum of previous monotheisms. Among later polemicists (not to mention modern Islamophobes) this led to the charge that Muhammad had simply copied his message from the preexistent monotheisms that he and his followers encountered. Though later Muslim tradition would try to get around this accusation by claiming that Muhammad was illiterate (*ummi*) – and thus unfamiliar with the scriptures of others – we nevertheless possess no formal evidence when it comes to what exactly the earliest Muslims knew of other religions. While the Quran, for example, mentions stories familiar to readers of the New and Old Testaments, it is by no means clear just what the relationship is between the Quran and these two earlier scriptures. There are, it should be duly noted, no verbatim quotations in the Quran of either the Jewish or the Christian scriptures. There are, then, polemical impulses in the claim that, depending on the metaphor employed, Islam is the byproduct or offspring of older and more stable monotheisms.

This narrative, and the evidence that supports it, is beset with so many historical problems as to be virtually untenable. While there certainly *may* be historical kernels to some of the stories that we possess, we must also appreciate that such kernels have been taken out of their original context and reshaped to meet new needs or functions. Most of our sources, for example, come from later, often much later, generations. These include the biography of Muhammad (*Sirat Rasul Allah*), to be discussed later, hadith (reports on the sayings and deeds of Muhammad), and the later commentary tradition on the Quran, known in Arabic as *tafsir*. Such sources would have been written in more cosmopolitan centers where more stable Muslims would have interacted with more stable Jews. We thus have to be cautious because both of these later identities were projected back onto the time of Muhammad.

This initial problem, in turn, generates many others. If we know very little about what transpired, for example, why should we simply assume that the Jews with whom Muhammad and his companions would have interacted were normative or rabbinic? Neither the Mishnah (which was codified in 200 CE) nor the Babylonian Talmud (codified ca. 500 CE), the two major works of rabbinic Judaism, mentions them. In addition, we have never found a copy of either of these works on the Arabian Peninsula that dates to the sixth or seventh century. While later sources may well claim that these Jews were normative and that they descended from Jerusalem, there is little evidence that we should take such accounts at face value. Many north Arabian inscriptions associated with these Jews, for example, lack any Jewish liturgical formulae or explicit symbols.[4] The later genealogist Ibn Kalbi (737–819) mentions that Jews of Medina married polytheists from the tribe of Quraysh in Mecca (the tribe from which Muhammad came). This would seem to contradict the notion, based on other later sources, that these Medinese Jews represented some sort of priestly oasis where Jewish elites assembled in the aftermath of the destruction of the Second Temple. Though, admittedly, Ibn Kalbi is also a later source, why should we believe those that make these Jews normative any more than his? For those like Goitein, these Jews represent a continuity between the Second Temple period and later rabbinic centers in places like Iraq.

Later Islamic sources written in Arabic, however, do not make up our only dataset. We also possess other accounts that, while also problematic, provide supplemental, if not alternative, versions of the period in question. These include earlier texts and inscriptions written in Syriac, Nabatean, Sabaic, and other languages common in the late antique Arabian Peninsula prior to the birth of Muhammad, which would have been replaced by Arabic after the advent of Islam. Though, of course, once again, we face the problem of how to read and contextualize them since they are often fragments written on stone or funerary inscriptions.

It is worth mentioning in the present context that all of the sources mentioned in the current chapter, both earlier and later, were not written as histories in the sense that we use this term today. Moreover, with few exceptions, claims of the authors (often anonymous) to the contrary, these sources are often not coterminous with the events upon which they purport to comment. Those that do provide us with more eyewitness accounts – such as tombstones, inscriptions, and graffiti – are so incomplete and often context-less as to make reconstruction, at least in the present, very difficult.

Pre-Islamic Arabia

Who then were the Jews that lived on the Arabian Peninsula just prior to and at the advent of Islam? The simple answer is that we are not entirely sure. Many, however, are content to make them rabbinic and have them responsible for the birth of Islam.[5] Very little, in other words, has changed since the pronouncement of the great nineteenth-century historian of the Jews, Heinrich Graetz (1817–1891). The Arabian Jews, according to him, while seemingly indistinct physically and culturally from their neighbors, were nevertheless religiously set apart from them.[6] Though ostensibly Arabs on the outside, for Graetz they nonetheless remained pure Jews on the inside.[7] We must be cautious, however, of retroactively reading the stability of later centuries back onto the period in question. This has tended to be our default position, and these later identities are subsequently used to compare so-called Jews and so-called Arabs or Muslims at a time when both were unstable social groups.

There are, to be sure, a number of problems that beset those trying to reconstruct Jewish life on the Arabian Peninsula. What we know about these Jews is, to reiterate, based on epigraphical evidence, contemporaneous external sources, and later Muslim sources – all of which are potentially problematic. Later rabbinic literature, as we have seen, never mentions them, and many of the early Muslim sources, discussed earlier, are anachronistic.

Despite the confidence of both (later) primary and secondary (including scholarly) sources that use the latter unproblematically into the present, we have very little idea of what Judaism looked like in these various regions on the Arabian Peninsula in the third or fourth century, let alone in the sixth when Muhammad comes on the scene of world history. Reading against the grain of our sources, I think it is safe to say that it is difficult to imagine that there was a normative Judaism at this period, let alone a normative Judaism on the Arabian Peninsula that existed far removed from what was simultaneously emerging as tannaitic Judaism in developing rabbinic centers such as Usha in the Galilee.

While we have little material evidence for grandiose narratives that tell us definitively who these Jews were, we do possess numerous tombstones, inscriptions, and graffiti.[8] There exists in Dedan, an oasis in central Arabia not far from Yathrib (Medina), for example, a tombstone erected by one Yahya bar Shimun for his father that dates to 307 CE.[9] Such an early date means, with certainty, that the people in question could not have been rabbinic Jews. There also exist numerous examples of graffiti in the area that would, again, appear to denote Jewish names. However, it is worth noting that many of these examples of graffiti are written in Nabataean (a dialect of Aramaic) or Arabic, and not Hebrew.[10] While such graffiti tells us that Jews were in the area, it unfortunately tells us little when it comes to where they came from, much less what exactly they believed.

The "Jews" of Himyar

We also know that there existed a Jewish kingdom in South Arabia, which corresponds roughly to modern day Yemen.[11] What we know about these Jews again largely derives from later Muslim sources and contemporaneous local inscriptions,[12] although here we are aided by the existence of external inscriptions (e.g., the *Monumentum Adulitanum*),[13] Christian hagiographies (e.g., the early sixth-century Syriac *Book of the Himyarites*), and other works (such as the fifth-century Anomean Philostorgius's *Ecclesiastical History*). Such sources tell us that at some point in the fourth century, the kingdom of Himyar seems to have converted to Judaism, perhaps not coincidentally about half a century after the conversion of the Ethiopian kingdom of Axum (just across the Red Sea) to a monophysite version of Christianity.[14] This Jewish kingdom lasted for roughly two centuries, until it was taken over by its Axumite rivals in the sixth century.[15] While our dominant narrative will say that these South Arabian Jews, like those Jews in the Hijaz (including Yathrib/Medina), provided the raw materials for the birth of Islam in the seventh century, the situation once again would seem to be much murkier on the ground.

South Arabia was home to, depending on the narrative, Jewish communities derived from Jewish exiles of Jerusalem and environs,[16] or autochthonous South Arabian clans professing some form of monotheism/Judaism. Rather than subscribe to or endorse either narrative, I prefer to use these communities as a mechanism to problematize "Judaism" in the late antique period and to reveal how these Himyarite Jews show with some degree of clarity just how difficult it is to neatly disentangle Judaism, the so-called religion, from other markers of identity, such as ethnicity, tribalism, or other political configurations.

While it is clear that the Himyarite kingdom converted to some form of Judaism based on numerous Sabaic inscriptions in the area, we have very little idea of the contents or contours of this "Judaism." Robin notes that around 380 CE inscriptions cease to reference the polytheistic deities of South Arabia, and begin to refer solely to Rahmanan ("the Merciful One").[17] Though these "post-conversion" inscriptions refer to a monotheistic deity, it is worth noting that they nonetheless remain in the Sabaic language of South Arabia and do not appear, for example, in either Hebrew or Aramaic. Some have argued that Rahmanan might be related to the Hebrew *rahamim* or a precursor to Allah, the high god of the North. But it is not at all clear if these, to use Beeston's locution, "Himyarite Rahmanists" in South Arabia are synonymous with "Jews," or indeed what monotheism even meant in this particular time and place. [18] Perhaps also significant is the fact that this presumably widespread conversion elicited no changes in the script, calendar, or language of the Himyarites.

Both the internal and external manuscript traditions – including from the later Islamic tradition – verify the existence of this Jewish kingdom.[19] Surprisingly, Jewish sources, particularly rabbinic ones, ignore it. There is no mention, as indicated, of any Himyarite king in either the Mishnah or the Talmud, which is significant since this would represent the first time since 70 CE that Jews possessed any sort of political autonomy.[20] Despite the absence of the Jews from canonical and normative sources, we possess inscriptions informing us of their identity as far away as Beth Shearim in the Galilee. A Hebrew inscription from Suar (modern day Jordan) from roughly 470 CE, for example, notes the burial of one Yosi b. Awfa.

This is the resting place of Yoseh b. Awfa, who died in the city of Tafar in the land of the Himyarites, leaving for the land of Israel and who was buried the day of the eve of Sabbath, the 29th day of month of Tammuz . . . equal to the year [400] of the destruction of Temple. Peace [Shalom].[21]

While the name Yosi is certainly attested in Jewish sources, the patronym Awfa is not and would seem to be of "Arab" derivation. So, who is

Yosi b. Awfa? An Arab Jew or a Jewish Arab? Or something entirely different? But even this raises as many questions as it answers. Was he, like many of the Himyarite Jews, a "convert"? If so, to which type of Judaism was he a convert? A later heterodox form of Judaism? If so, does this account for the relative silence in later Jewish sources?[22] Even more speculatively we might ask how does the emergence of Islam relate to such heterodox forms of Judaism? Another burial inscription, from roughly the same time period, this time in both Aramaic and Sabaic, reads as follows:

Aramaic

Here lies Leah, daughter of Judah. May her soul [rest] for the life eternal and may she be [ready] for the resurrection at the end of days. Amen and amen. Shalom.

Sabaic

Here lies Leah, daughter of Yawdah. May Rahmanan allow her rest. Amen. Shalom.[23]

As Robin notes this inscription is interesting in the sense that the Aramaic version denotes the afterlife and gives no name of the deity, whereas the Sabaic version mentions the deity's name (the aforementioned Rahmanan) but fails to make any mention of the afterlife.[24]

I have mentioned these two inscriptions because, like other ones from this time and place, they push us to rethink just what we know (and do not) about Judaism and Jewish history at this particular period. Such inscriptions, and the questions to which they give rise, would seem to complicate the operative model that posits a normative and rabbinic Jewish community on the Peninsula. There is no good reason, in other words, to assume that what is going on in amoraic academies is normative and binding on all Jews at this point in time.

Muhammad

It seems that it was Jews like this – non-normative, theologically inchoate, liturgically and doctrinally in flux – with whom Muhammad and his earliest followers would have interacted. They were not, in other words, the rabbinic and normative Jews of later centuries. The next question, of course, becomes what was the nature of such interactions?

Once again, we remain on unstable terrain. What we possess are often much later stories that describe these interactions. While such stories may well help us understand how later generations understood the relationship between Muslims and Jews, they unfortunately provide very little insight into their actual relations. If anything, these later sources complicate our understanding because, ever since their appearance, they have been presented – and more often than not received – as if they were eyewitness accounts of what actually happened.

It is imperative, however, not to assume that these texts are transcripts of events that actually transpired. Instead, we ought to contextualize such stories as a way that the subsequent Muslim community imagined itself, doing so, moreover, using the trope of "the Jews." The latter category could then function as a catalyst for Muslim self-definition. If the Jews were imagined to do or say "x," for example, the Muslims did "y." More often than not this involved invoking the "Jew" as a trope for stubbornness or resistance – not unlike the trope of "Pharisaic" functions in early Christianity – to Muhammad's prophetic call. "Jews," thus, became a convenient marker by which subsequent Muslim ideas could be articulated.[25]

Despite the later invocation of such tropes, however, it is perhaps more apposite to think of the earliest Muslims and Jews as indistinct from one another. In a relatively recent monograph titled *Muhammad and the Believers*, Fred Donner refers to the earliest community as "Believers" (*muminun*) as opposed to Muslims (*muslimun*) on account of the lack of firm doctrinal, liturgical, and ritualist components, which would be developed only in later centuries. While at the beginning Jews, Muslims, Christians, and other monotheists would have had much in common with one another and would most likely have been indistinct from one another, as the decades progressed, so-called framers of Islam – namely, legists, theologians, hadith collectors, and so on – would have gradually differentiated these Believers into discrete communities, to wit, "Jews" and "Muslims."

Again, and unlike the case with an earlier generation of Orientalists, this is not to make the claim that "Islam" was underdefined in these early years and that Judaism was somehow a stable and well-defined religious tradition that was complete with its own set of religious doctrines and beliefs. As we have already seen in this chapter, it is anything but clear who these Jews were, and it is more profitable to imagine them as equally fluid. This fluidity would in the ensuing years lead to gradual self-definition on the part of each community. Two things we should keep in mind, however. The first is that each needed the other to undertake this self-definition. Each community, in other words, derived energy and the need for self-definition from the other. Second, this does not mean, especially in the early decades, that there were no communities who were both Jewish and Muslim, as we shall see later, in terms of at least some of their beliefs.

Quran

The Quran invokes many biblical stories, undoubtedly contributing to the impression that Muhammad or the final redactors of the Quran were familiar with Jewish and Christian scriptures. However, the Quran does not take up these themes in the same kind of sustained narrative found in these other sources. When it does mention such earlier stories, it is more interested in the religious message than actual narrative details. Because of its arrangement, from longest to shortest suras, as opposed to thematic or chronological organization, the Quran appears to lack any real beginning, middle, or end, with the result that there is very little narrative continuity in the work. This, needless to say, makes any type of synoptic comparison between the Quran and both the Old and New Testaments difficult.

Moreover, terms such as "borrowing" and "influencing" may not adequately account for the historical, religious, and literary context of seventh-century Arabia. Themes such as desert dwellers, illiterate prophets, revelation and persecution, and the hope for ultimate redemption form part of a larger Near Eastern cultural legacy. In this regard, "borrowing" from a shared cultural matrix is not necessarily borrowing at all, but instead using a set of preexistent and common discourses to articulate particular situations. Read on this level, the Quran is not simply the sum of its parts but shares in a broader Near Eastern religious and mythic heritage. Consider, for example, the Quranic version of the flood story, which essentially becomes an altogether new Islamic story:

> We sent Noah to his people, saying,
> "Warn your people, before a painful punishment comes upon them."
> He said, "O my people,
> I am a clear warner to you.
> Serve God and fear Him, and obey me,

And He will forgive you some of your sins and defer you to a stated
term.
God's term, when it comes, cannot be deferred
If you did but know it."
[Noah] said, "My Lord,
I have summoned my people night and day,
But my summoning has increased them only in flight
Whenever I summon them so that You might forgive them,
they put their fingers in their ears
and draw their garments over them
and persist and are full of pride."

(71: 1–8)

Although the name "Noah" is certainly familiar, as is the basic narrative presupposed in it, the emphasis on the sending of a prophet, the people's unwillingness to listen to him, and their gradual destruction are much different from what we encounter in other Near Eastern flood stories, such as in the Epic of Gilgamesh or even in the Bible.

What do we do with such stories? Do we assume that the Quran simply "copies" stories found in earlier scriptures? This has tended to be the default position. Despite this, however, there is no verbatim quotation of the Old or New Testaments in the Quran. Do we assume, as others do, that the early community was somehow aware of extra-canonical sources (e.g., *midrashim*, that is, interpretive stories popular in rabbinic Judaism)?[26] But we surely have to be aware that such an argument also has the potential to work in the other direction. Again, given the common Near Eastern heritage and the fluidity of terms within rabbinic Judaism and Islam in the seventh and eighth centuries there is reason to assume that redactors of the Quran might well have "influenced" the formation of rabbinic legend as much as vice versa. For example, some of the rabbinic collections detailing these extrabiblical narratives postdate the compilation of the Quran.

Muhammad and the Jews of Medina

When Muhammad moved (*hijra*) from Mecca to Medina on account of persecution in the former desert oasis, the situation between him and some of the Jewish tribes of Medina deteriorated fairly quickly in his new home. Although normative Jewish tradition forbade the existence of new prophets and lawgivers, there is no reason not to believe that other types of Judaism were open to messianic figures and movements. At any rate, it was around this time that some of these Jewish tribes were accused of conspiring with Muhammad's enemies in Mecca to overthrow him. Muhammad confronted these tribes and gave one, the Banu Qurayza, a choice between conversion and death, and they seem to have chosen the latter. Later accounts tell that all the men of this tribe were murdered and their wives and children sold into slavery. Islamophobic commentators continue to use this story as "evidence" of Muhammad's anti-Semitism. However, it is worth pointing out that other sources mention the existence of Jewish–Arab tribes in Medina long after the Banu Qurayza's alleged treason. Sources also tell us that the sanction imposed on the Banu Qurayza was decided on in consultation with Jewish–Arab tribal leaders. Finally, there exists no corroborating evidence as to the historicity of these events outside of Muslim sources; as a consequence, we are on no firmer historical ground when discussing these events than when discussing anything else alleged to have transpired during the early period of Islam.

The later biographical literature, however, has the following to say about the Jewish tribes of Medina:

> About this time the Jewish rabbis showed hostility to the apostle in envy, hatred, and malice, because God had chosen His apostle from the Arabs. They were joined by men from al-Aus and al-Khazraj who had obstinately clung to their heathen religion. They were hypocrites, clinging to the polytheism of their fathers denying the resurrection; yet when Islam appeared and their people flocked to it they were compelled to pretend to accept it to save their lives. But in secret they were hypocrites whose inclination was towards the Jews because they considered the apostle a liar and strove against Islam. . . . It was the Jewish rabbis who used to annoy the apostle with questions and introduce confusion, so as to confound the truth with falsity. The Quran used to come down in reference to these questions of theirs, though some of the questions about what was allowed and forbidden came from the Muslims themselves.[27]

Later Muslim tradition suggests that it was around this time that the Quran (e.g., 2:112, 5:56, 9:182) began to speak of the Jews (*al-yahud*) in negative terms, often associating them with hypocrites (*al-munafiqun*).

Most important for Islamic self-definition, it was also around this time that Muhammad (the biographical tradition says God) switched the *qibla*, or direction of prayer, for his followers from Jerusalem to Mecca, told his followers not to rest on the Jewish Sabbath, and instituted the fast at Ramadan to replace Yom Kippur. It is such acts – whether or not they happened in such a dramatic fashion is, of course, impossible to verify – wherein we see clearly the need of the early Muslim community to differentiate itself from those of the Jews.

The biography of Muhammad

An important early text that seeks to begin this process of differentiating Muslims from Jews in light of such fluidity is the aforementioned *Sirat Rasul Allah*, literally "the Biography of God's Messenger." As both a specific text and a subsequent genre, it seeks to offer a narrative account of Muhammad's life, often including miraculous and other such events that can be attributed to him. Along with collections of hadith – that is, the sayings and deeds of Muhammad recorded by his companions and handed down to posterity – the *Sira* both constructs and constitutes the "way" or exemplary life, known in Arabic as the *Sunnah*, of Muhammad. It is this *Sunnah* that subsequently forms the basis of, among other things, Islamic law and practice.

The *Sira* is not, desires of believers to the contrary, a historical biography. It is instead a hagiography and, as such, must be read accordingly. It is quite literally an attempt to write a sacred biography of an individual whom the early community knew very little about, yet about whom they wanted to know a great deal. Indeed, it is the *Sira* literature that succeeds in establishing a prophetic personality in order to connect it to and make sense of what was slowly emerging as the normative Quranic narrative. The *Sira* thus became a central component in establishing the relevant contexts of revelation – the so-called *asbab al-nuzul*, as they are known in Arabic – for the early and fledgling Muslim community to make sense of themselves and their emerging religion in ways that enfolded a personality-less divine revelation into a series of quasi-historical and quasi-miraculous episodes of Muhammad's life. This would be both an important and necessary endeavor in a highly cosmopolitan and religiously competitive environment like Baghdad, where Muslims encountered and interacted with other monotheists, both Jews and Christians, who were in possession of their own religious scriptures and, especially, oral traditions associated with their prophets that helped them to make sense of their religious worldviews.

Muslims would have had but a very recent tradition of both their scripture and prophetic stories about it. In such a rich and competitive marketplace of ideas, the framers and articulators of early Islam needed equally miraculous tales of their founder, and, simultaneously, they also needed a religious pedigree for themselves. They inevitably sought to create or collect stories that were similar in both content and form to those that other religious traditions would have possessed. It is within this context that we must imagine the *Sira* as helping to construct and subsequently legitimate prophetic authority in early Islam by giving the young Muslim community a prophet in a familiar biblical or Near Eastern mold. This is certainly not to say that the early framers of Islam sought to copy or otherwise plagiarize stories, but it is to claim that they reworked a set of familiar tropes, biblical and otherwise, to make sense of their prophet and ultimately themselves.

The earliest biography of Muhammad – the *Sirat Rasul Allah* by Ibn Ishaq (704–ca. 770), which survives only in the recension by Ibn Hisham (d. 833) – is by no means coeval with its subject matter. These surviving accounts, then, date to roughly 150 to 200 years after 632 CE, the year that the Muslim tradition ascribes to the death of Muhammad. The *Sirat Rasul Allah* appears at a crucial moment in the formation of Islam, and it represents an important intervention in that formation.

Ibn Ishaq was the grandson of a Persian war captive brought to Medina, and was subsequently educated by his father, who was a collector of stories about Muhammad, some of which would be used in hadith transmission. As a young man, Ibn Ishaq moved to the Abbasid capital, the new city of Baghdad, where he quickly found important patrons in the new regime. The caliph al-Mansur, for example, employed him as a tutor and commissioned him to write an all-encompassing history from the creation of the world to the present. This work, which he wrote but which does not survive, was divided into three sections: "al-Mubtada" dealing with creation up to Arabian pre-Islamic history; "al-Mabath" from pre-Islamic Arabia to the birth of Muhammad; and "al-Maghazi" that includes what we might call the more traditional biography of Muhammad. This grand narrative, thus, was an attempt to situate Muhammad and the early Muslim polity as the centerpiece of world history. In order to write such a book, however, Ibn Ishaq had to employ stories derived from Jews and Christians, a genre known by the name "Israiliyyat," many of which are versions of non-canonical stories that early Muslims would have undoubtedly heard from Jews, quasi-Jews, and/or others in their midst.[28]

Why did Ibn Ishaq's broad-based and all-encompassing history not survive? It seems that, as Gordon Newby duly notes, in the generation immediately after Ibn Ishaq, the genre of Israiliyyat fell into disrepute, most likely because it was identified with rival monotheisms, especially Judaism, at a time when those entrusted with the articulation of Islam were attempting to extricate the new religion from these earlier ones.[29] Ibn Ishaq thus employed what would later become a problematic if not forbidden set of narrative units. His *Sira*, thus, had a paradoxical role in this formation: on the one hand it helped to create a sense of community that was emerging from a period of social and intellectual fluidity, but, on the other, it was precisely this fluidity, especially the danger of a retreat back into it, that threatened to undermine the new community.

This means that subsequent recensions of *Sirat Rasul Allah*, especially the later one by Ibn Hisham, played a formative role in the creation of what was slowly emerging as a discrete tradition at a time when some were worried that Ibn Ishaq's original biography had showed Islam's debt to other religions and, in so doing, blurred lines between Muslims and others. Stories that were now seen as too "Jewish" were frowned upon if not actually banned, even though such stories seemed to have been seen as fine a generation earlier. In the movement from Ibn Ishaq's *Sira* to Ibn Hisham's *Sira*, a span of about 50 years, we witness a sea-change in Muslim self-perception. If Ibn Ishaq's work was seen as too Jewish, Ibn Hisham's was an attempt to separate that which was now perceived to be Islamic from that which was now imagined to be Jewish.

Ibn Hisham's *Sira*, thus, represents the end of the fluidity of early Islam and the movement toward what will eventually become a more fixed boundary between Islam and other monotheisms. Rather than connect Muhammad to the salvation histories of other traditions as Ibn Ishaq's original seems to have done, Ibn Hisham's recension succeeded in creating a supersessionist religious tradition, one wherein Muhammad becomes the seal of the prophets and his message, Islam, becomes the legal and spiritual fulfillment of previous religious traditions. Its motive, then, is as much political as it is religious, realizing, of course, that the political and the religious cannot be neatly separated from one another at the end of late antiquity. The movement from Ibn Ishaq's *Sira* to that of Ibn Hisham thus reveals a significant turning point in the history of early Islam.

The *Sira*, then, quite literally constructs Islam's prophet. He is, after all, only rarely mentioned in the Quran and certainly with no indication of his idiosyncratic personality traits. The early biographical literature attempts to create the life of the man who had become or who was in the process of becoming most associated with divine revelation in Islam. Indeed, some might even go so far as to argue that the biographical tradition in Islam fleshed out an individual because the later Islamic tradition needed such a life to make sense of the book. The *Sira* literature, therefore, is an early attempt at historicization: to historicize divine revelation in the narrative context of a human life.[30] In this respect, the main goal of the biography is to establish and explain the various contexts wherein Muhammad was *imagined* to have received the specifics of the Quran's revelation, contexts that tradition records as lasting over a 20-year period.

Because of this, the *Sira* is, to repeat, not a work of history, but one of hagiography. It is thus the work of creative storytellers or myth makers seeking both to understand and to explain Muhammad – and thus themselves – in light of narratives that they inherited from a common Near Eastern religious, literary, and cultural heritage. The stories that we encounter in this early biographical tradition reveal as much about those who created them as they do about Muhammad. Written in cosmopolitan centers, such as Baghdad and Cairo, the *Sira* is an attempt on the part of the early framers of Islam to begin the process of differentiating what was slowly emerging as a normative Islamic tradition from other monotheisms in the same places and locales. Again, it connects Islam to a larger message, but in the process shows how its iteration is the most superior form of that message. The *Sira* is an attempt to firm Islam up in centers where such firming up was both possible and necessary. In this respect, we need to situate the *Sira* as a later and more stable attempt to impose order on an earlier and much more ambiguous social situation.

Let me now provide a few examples of the way in which the *Sirat Rasul Allah* establishes the authority of the Prophet Muhammad over the community of believers (*umma*) as it simultaneously distances his message from that of "the Jews." One such example is the beginning of the *Sira*, which, not unlike the first chapter of the Gospel of Matthew, seeks to connect the genealogy of the prophet to Adam *via* Abraham, only now through the son Ishmael as opposed to Isaac. Muhammad, not unlike Jesus, becomes the messianic fulfillment of biblical prophecy. Or, again, in another story recounting Muhammad's birth, the *Sira* describes Islam's prophet in the following terms:

> Amina bint Wahb, the mother of God's apostle, used to say when she was pregnant with God's apostle that a voice would say to her, "You are pregnant with the lord of this people and when he is born say that, 'I will put him in the care of the One and away from the evil of every envier; then call him Muhammad.'" As she was pregnant with him she saw a light come forth from her by which she could see the castles of Busra in Syria.[31]

Busra, it is perhaps worth noting, was the capital of the Ghassanid king-dom of Arab-Christians and a vassal of the Byzantine Empire. In 634, according to tradition, the early Muslim forces captured it, making the city one of the first important Byzantine cities to be captured. In a later section, these so-called enviers are constructed in a way that they become synonymous with Jews, who are increasingly seen as problematic or as a threat to Muhammad's well-being in this literature. For example, Abu Talib, the young Muhammad's uncle and guardian, meets a monk by the name of Bahira in the desert, who is described as "being well-versed in the knowledge of Christians" – but interestingly not in that of the Jews – and in possession of a book that had been handed down to him "from generation to generation."[32] When Bahira looks at the young Muhammad's back he sees "the seal of prophecy between his shoulders in the very place described in his book."[33] Bahira then informs Abu Talib, "Take your nephew back to his country and guard him carefully against the Jews, for by Allah! If they see him and know about him what I know, they will do him evil: a great future lies before this nephew of yours, so take him home quickly." Bahira thus functions as a monotheist who is able to legitimate Muhammad's prophecy as he simultaneously differen-tiates Muhammad from "the Jews."

Here, once again, we see later discrete lines between religions placed retroactively onto the period that is here synonymous with Muhammad's childhood, a time when Islam did not even exist yet. Muslims and Islam, in other words, had to be made distinct from other social groups and reli-gions at a time when they would have been anything but discrete.

One final example should suffice. Ibn Hisham's *Sira* also mentions Jewish rabbis who had accepted Islam hypocritically. "These hypocrites (*al-munafiqun*)," so we learn, "used to assemble in the mosque and listen to the stories of the Muslims and laugh and scoff at their religion."[34] Again, this is an early, and I think we could say anachronistic, attempt to differentiate Muslims and Islam from Jews and Judaism. There was, for example, no clear or distinct message of Islam that one could have converted to in the earliest years since such a message would be worked out only by subsequent generations of legists. It is also significant that in this story we now begin to see "Jews" (*al-yahud*) and "hypocrites" used interchangeably with one another. Despite this, however, the *Sira* still needs to connect Muhammad to the biblical paradigm as a way to make sense of him and, just as importantly, for others to make sense of him as well. It is in this light that we must see and situate the stories of Muhammad's preaching to the Bedouin, emigration to Medina, and so forth. All have biblical precedents and help Muslims to understand the prophetic career of Muhammad.

The *Sira* functions as the primary means whereby Islam's prophet is constructed, imagined, and subsequently disseminated at a formative moment of the fledgling community's existence. In so doing, it transforms the Prophet Muhammad into a biblical-type prophet, but a duly noted superior version of such a prophet, something that would have been necessary in a cosmopolitan milieu such as Baghdad, which functioned as a highly competitive intellectual and monotheistic environment. The *Sira* thus plays a seminal role in legitimizing the new religious movement, providing flesh to its bones. Moreover, it also functions as a polemical text that attempts to show the miraculous nature of Muhammad's life and thereby establishes his authority over other prophets. This was certainly connected to the desire on the part of the framers of the early community to show the superiority of Muhammad – and by extension his text and his religion – over that of rival prophetic figures, such as Moses and Jesus, and their religions. If before the nascent community was content to live in an intellectual environment that appreciated the interconnections and ecumenicism between monotheisms, by the end of the eighth century, firm lines had to be drawn between them.

Non-canonical texts

In addition to canonical texts such as the Quran, hadith, and *Sira* literature, we also possess a body of literature from the seventh and eighth centuries that is directly relevant to the period in question. Many of these texts are from non-Islamic sources and are of interest because they bear witness to variant traditions that the later canonical narrative of Islam displaced.[35] The result is a set of texts that reveal the sort of porousness that is familiar to many who conduct work in the late antique period. My goal in surveying these sources is not to be exhaustive, but only to suggest what can occur when we situate early Islam within a larger late antique context as opposed to just projecting later sources back onto the period in question.

One of the earliest extant texts to mention Muhammad is an anti-Jewish Christian treatise written in Greek (though it also survives in Ethiopic, Arabic, and Church Slavonic) that narrates events claimed to have taken place in the 630s. The text, known as the *Doctrina Iacoba*, recounts a dialogue between Jacob, a Jewish merchant from Palestine who had recently been forced to convert to Christianity, and a group of Jews, in which they discuss the condition of the Byzantine Empire in light of the recent Arab conquest. At one point in the dialogue, Jacob mentions the arrival of a new prophet in Palestine:

> When the Saracens killed the *candidatus* [i.e., Sergios, commander of the Byzantine army in Palestine], I was at Caesarea and I set off by boat to Sykmania [near the modern city of Haifa]. People were saying "the candidatus has been killed," and we Jews were over-joyed. And they were saying that the prophet had appeared, coming with the Saracens, and that he was proclaiming the advent of the anointed one, the Christ who was to come.[36]

This passage is interesting for a number of reasons. First, and most importantly for my purposes, it shows how the three monotheisms are not entirely separate from one another at this point in history. They are all interconnected and porous, sharing the same literal and metaphorical vocabulary. Muhammad is here described apocalyptically as the harbinger of the "Christos," in such a way that a rather generic late antique apocalypticism encompasses Jews, Christians, *and* Muslims. It is surely significant that one of the earliest non-Muslim references to Muhammad's message describes him as preaching a message of Jewish messianism.[37] This is further evidence that, at least in its earliest decades, and prior to the emergence of a fully theologically fleshed out Islam, the tradition seems to have absorbed and reworked a number of ideas and tropes shared by others, including a sense of the apocalypse and the importance of Jerusalem and the so-called Holy Land. Second, it shows how some of the earliest witnesses to Muhammad's prophetic message were Jews, again remembering that this descriptor might well be under-defined at this point.[38] Finally, and less important for my purposes here, but nevertheless of interest, is the implication that Muhammad was alive during the invasion of Palestine, something that the normative tradition does not mention.

In other texts, we see even more clearly this idea that Jews under-stood Muhammad and his message as the fulfillment of Jewish messian-ism. One such text is the mid-eighth-century *Secrets of Rabbi Shimon bar Yohai*.[39] This ostensibly Jewish work, written during the period of upheaval associated with the end of the Umayyad dynasty and the begin-ning of the Abbasid dynasty, again identifies Muhammad as the fulfill-ment of Jewish messianic speculation. Like the *Doctrina Iacoba*, this text offers further evidence of how contemporaneous Jews understood the early Islamic conquests.[40] The *Secrets of Rabbi Shimon bar Yohai* goes even further than the latter work, however, in its presentation of Muhammad as the fulfillment of Jewish messianic speculation. The work ends with the desire for the restoration of the Temple in Jerusalem and the hope that the Abbasid revolution will usher in an apocalyptic battle between Israel and Byzantium, followed by the Final Judgment. Near the beginning of the text, Metatron, an individual who figures highly in both Jewish and Islamic angelology,[41] informs Rabbi Shimon that,

> because of [Byzantium's] oppression of Israel, the Holy One, blessed be He, sends Ishmaelites against them, who make war against them in order to save Israel from their hands. Then a crazy man possessed by a spirit arises and speaks lies about the Holy One, blessed be He, and he conquers the land, and there is enmity between them and the sons of Esau.[42]

This ostensibly "Jewish" document recycles Muslim apocalyptic spec-ulation, some of which had already been paradoxically recycled from Jewish sources by early Muslims. Again, rather than perceiving this as borrowing or influence, we should see it as collective worldmaking in an environment wherein ideas moved freely across porous boundaries. The result is that it is impossible to know with any degree of precision what is "Jewish" and what is "Muslim." In "light of the confessional boundar-ies that have long since separated Islam and Judaism," writes Stephen J.

Shoemaker, "recent research into Islamic origins has revealed that such divisions were likely not as important during Islam's first decades."[43]

In yet another text, the *History of the Patriarchs of Alexandria*, written in the 710s,[44] we read of Muhammad in the following terms:

> There arose a man from the Arabs, from the southern regions, from Mecca and its vicinity, named Muhammad. And he restored the worshippers of idols to knowledge of the one God, so that they said that Muhammad is his messenger. And his nation was circumcised in the flesh, not in the law, and they prayed toward the south, orientating themselves toward a place they call the Kaaba. And he took possession of Damascus and Syria, and he crossed the Jordan and dammed it up. And the Lord abandoned the army of the Romans before him, because of their corrupt faith and the excommunication that was brought against them and because of the Council of Chalcedon by the ancient fathers.[45]

This text is interesting because, like the *Secrets of Rabbi Shimon bar Yohai*, it presents Muhammad and his message in nonpolemical terms. The text, the product of the monophysite Coptic Church, speaks of how Muhammad received divine favor on account of the piety of his actions, including that of leading the Arabs to monotheism. If anything, the text reserves its animus for the Council of Chalcedon (451 CE), which resulted – according to the text's authors – in the divine favor being removed from Byzantine Christianity.

Again, it is worth underscoring that all of these texts are the products of late antiquity, against which they must be contextualized and understood. If anything they reveal the complexity of socio-religious identities, just as they simultaneously illumine how narratives from Judaism, Christianity, and Islam are invested in one another. Such texts, none of which are explicitly "Muslim," nonetheless reveal quite a lot about Islam. In this regard, Muhammad and the early Muslims tapped into, as Jews and Christians did, a common stock of tropes and motifs.[46] It would be incorrect to say that one group possessed these to the exclusion of others. The early Muslims, in other words, did not borrow their ideas from Judaism. Rather, Muslims consciously and creatively reimagined their world using a vocabulary they shared with other monotheisms. These Islamic rereadings were consonant with the decentralized pluralism associated with late antiquity.

Constitution of Medina

It might well be worth mentioning the so-called Constitution of Medina in this context. This Constitution, often attributed to Muhammad (who was, according to tradition, illiterate), has been described, perhaps apologetically, as "The First Written Constitution in the World."[47] Though it is assumed to date to the first year after his *hijra* (622 CE), or "exodus," from Mecca when Muhammad had been invited by the inhabitants of Yathrib/Medina to be a lawmaker among quarreling tribes there, the earliest copy we possess dates to at least a century after Muhammad's presence there.

Regardless, Michael Lecker, who assumes the text to be authentic, notes that although 11 "Jewish" tribes are mentioned, the three main ones (Nadir, Qurayza, and Qaynuqa) are not. He also argues that by this time the Jews of Arabia would have been included in the Constitution as clients of the Ansar ("helpers," namely, of the earliest Muslims who came to live in Medina), among whom they lived. Interestingly, again according to Lecker, one of the tribes explicitly mentioned in the Constitution, the Thalaba, seem to have been a "Jewish" tribe composed of Arab converts.[48] The existence of tribes like the Thalaba, then, reveals further just how fluid the line between Muslim and Jew was in this early period. Did such groups convert to "Judaism" – once again, remembering that what this term meant at this time and in this place is difficult to determine – or was this, as with the *Sira* literature, a later retrojection? Or did this tribe convert to a form of monotheism that, again, only in retrospect would be recognized as a form distinct from what would emerge as Islam? Regardless, we see once again just how difficult it is to differentiate between Muslim and Jew in this early period. Those texts that do seek to differentiate between them, moreover, seem to date to later periods when such differences were both important and, because of this, necessary to put onto the earliest period. Our mistake, to reiterate, is to take these later stories as if they provide eyewitness accounts to the events in question.

Conclusions

This chapter has presented a historical overview of the earliest years of Jewish-Muslim interactions, from roughly the time of Muhammad until the years immediately following his death. This timeframe, as I have alluded to time and again, is shrouded in mystery. Though some would go so far as to say that, because of this, we are unable to know anything at all about the period in question, I have opted for a more sanguine approach. While these texts are problematic and many date from later periods, they nevertheless betray a fluidity between social groups that should be familiar to those who conduct work into the late antique period.

Within this context, we should imagine Jews and Muslims in this early period as part of a shared monotheistic environment. Rather than call it "Jewish" or "Muslim," it might be more accurate to imagine this mono-theism as more ecumenical or open-ended than the later world religions paradigm can account for. Only gradually, as Islam came to be defined and articulated – theologically, legally, doctrinally, and ritually – did the boundaries between Jews and Muslims begin to be firmer and, eventu-ally, more stable. At this point, as I tried to argue, we are able to wit-ness these later lines of separation projected back onto the early period. Despite this, however, we would do well not to mistake or even mislabel the projection for the reality.

Notes

1 In addition to the work by Goitein cited in the Preface, see Heinrich Graetz, *History of the Jews* (Philadelphia: Jewish Publication Society of America, 1956 [1856]), vol. 3; Abraham Geiger, *Judaism and Islam*, trans. F. M. Young (Madras: MDCSPK Press, 1835; repr. New York: Ktav, 1970); Eli-yahu Ashtor, *The Jews of Moslem Spain*, trans. Aaron Klein and Jenny Machlowitz Klein (Philadelphia: Jewish Publication Society of America, 1973–84), 3 vols.; Norman Stillman, *The Jews of Arab Lands: A History and a Sourcebook* (Philadelphia: Jewish Publication Society of America, 1979); Newby, *A History of the Jews of Arabia*; Mazuz, *The Religious and Spiritual Life of the Jews of Medina*.

2 In Islamic Studies circles, this is known as the "Authenticity Debate." There exist at least three different perspectives in this debate. The first contends that even though the earliest sources of Islam may come from a later period, they nonetheless represent reasonably reliable accounts concerning the matters upon which they comment or describe. Another perspective contends that the Muslim historical record of the first two centuries is historically problematic. The social and political upheavals associated with the rapid spread of Islam fatally compromise, according to such scholars, the earliest sources. These sources, according to this position, are written so much after the fact and with such distinct ideological or political agendas that they provide us with very little that is reliable and with which to re-create the period that they purport to describe. The third perspective acknowledges the problems involved with the early sources, but tries to solve them using form and source criticism, both of

which seek to determine the original form and historical context of a particular text. A survey and analysis of these competing positions may be found in Herbert Berg, *The Development of Exegesis in Early Islam: The Authenticity of Muslim Literature From the Formative Period* (London: Curzon, 2000), 6–64.

3 Indeed Talya Fishman argues that this did not occur until as late as the Middle Ages. See her *Becoming the People of the Talmud: Oral Torah as Written Tradition in Medieval Jewish Cultures* (Philadelphia: University of Pennsylvania Press, 2011).

4 Christian Robin, "Ḥimyar et Israël," *Comptes-Rendus de l'Académie des Inscriptions et Belles-Lettres* (2004): 831–908, at 842.

5 Haggai Mazuz, for example, can opine (without a shred of evidence) that: "Our findings demonstrate that the Medinan Jews were Talmudic-Rabbinic Jews in almost every respect. Their sages believed in using homiletic Interpretation (*derash*) of the Scriptures, as did the sages of the Talmud. On many halakhic issues, their observations were identical to those of the Talmudic sages. In addition, they held Rabbinic beliefs, sayings, and motifs derived from Midrashic literature." See Mazuz, *The Religious and Spiritual Life of the Jews of Medina*, 99.

6 Graetz, *History of the Jews*, 3: 56.

7 Graetz, *History of the Jews*, 3: 58.

8 One of the earliest is a family tomb erected in 42 CE that comes from Hegra (roughly 50 km to the northwest of Yathrib). See John Healey, *The Nabataean Tomb Inscriptions of Mad'in Salih* (Oxford: JSS, 1993), no. 4.

9 E.g., Antonin Juasson and Rafaël Savignac, *Mission archéologique en Arabie* (Paris: E. Leroux, 1909–22), No. 386.

10 Most of the pre-Islamic Arab sources are found in inscriptions and papyri. See, e.g., Healey, *The Nabataean Tomb Inscriptions of Mad'in Salih*; Abu l-Hasan, *Qira'a li-kitabat Lihyaniyya min Jabal Akma bi-mantiqat al-Ula* (Riyad: King Fahd National Library, 1997); *Routes d'Arabie: Archéologie et Histoire du Royaume d'Arabie Saoudite*, eds. Ali Ibrahim al-Ghabban et al. (Paris: Somogy, 2010). On the non-Muslim sources, see Robert Hoyland, *Seeing Islam as Others Saw It: A Survey and Evaluation of Christian, Jewish, and Zoroastrian Writings on Early Islam* (Princeton: Darwin Press, 1997).

11 See Newby, *A History of the Jews of Arabia*, 33–48.

12 See, especially, Robin, "Ḥimyar et Israël," 831–908.

13 Glen W. Bowersock, *The Throne of Adulis: Red Sea Wars on the Eve of Islam* (New York: Oxford University Press, 2013). Though see also Pseudo-Dionysus of Tel-Mahre, *Chronicle II*, ed. J. B. Chabot (Paris: CSCO, 1933), translated by Witold Witakowski (Liverpool: Liverpool University Press, 1996), 54–56. See also George Hatke, *Aksum and Nubia: Warfare, Commerce, and Political Fictions in Ancient Northeast Africa* (New York: New York University Press, 2013).

14 Indeed, as Nebes suggests, it is "quite understandable to find the Ḥimyar joining the other form of monotheism a short time later, if only as an ideological countermeasure against their traditional Aksumite rivals and in order to stem the growing influence of the Byzantine Empire in the region." See Norbert Nebes, "The Martyrs of Najrān and the End of Ḥimyar: On the Political

History of South Arabia in the Early Sixth Century," in *The Qur'ān in Context: Historical and Literary Investigations Into the Qur'anic Milieu*, ed. Angelika Neuwirth, Nicolai Sinai, and Michael Marx (Leiden: Brill, 2010), 27–59, at 39–40.

15 Nebes, "The Martyrs of Najrān and the End of Ḥimyar," 48–52. See also Iwona Gajda, *Le royaume de Ḥimyar à l'époque monothéiste* (Paris: Académie des Inscriptions et Belles-Lettres, 2009), ch. 5.

16 Reuben Ahroni, *Yemenite Jewry: Origins, Culture and Literature* (Bloomington: Indiana University Press, 1986), 47–48.

17 See Robin, "Ḥimyar et Israël," 833.

18 "Rahmanan," for example, is also used in the largely Christian Syriac to refer to God. See Jakob Levy, *Chaldäisches Wörterbuch über die Targumim und einen grossen Teil des rabbinischen Schrifthums*, 2 vols (Leipzig: Verlag von Baumgärtner's Buchhandlung, 1876–89), vol. 2, 417b.

19 See Robin, "Ḥimyar et Israël," 833–835.

20 See Nebes, "The Martyrs of Najrān and the End of Ḥimyar," 39n56.

21 For a facsimile, see Joseph Naveh,"Seven New Epitaphs from Zoar" (Hebrew), *Tarbiz* LXIX (1999–2000): 619–635.

22 Here I differ from Newby, who argues that these "Arabian Jews were rabbinic in that they were organized into congregations headed by rabbis, and they were in touch, at least limitedly, with the Babylonian academies." But then he acknowledges, and in this sense I agree with him, that "it is clear that practices and beliefs of the Arabian Jews were different from the Judaism idealized in the Babylonian Talmud." See Gordon D. Newby, "The Jews of Arabia at the Birth of Islam," in *A History of Jewish-Muslim Relations: From Their Origins to the Present Day*, eds. Abdelwahab Meddeb and Benjamin Stora (Princeton: Princeton University Press, 2013), 39–51, at 39.

23 Robin, "Ḥimyar et Israël," 891. Facsimile of inscription may be found in Joseph Naveh, "A Bilingual Burial Inscription From Saba," *Leshonenu* LXV, no. 2 (2003): 117–120.

24 Robin, "Ḥimyar et Israël," 840.

25 This is not unlike the point that Mazuz tries to make. However, I cannot endorse his larger claim that these Jews were normative rabbinic Jews.

26 See Geiger, *Judaism and Islam*, or, more recently, James L. Kugle, *In Potiphar's House: The Interpretive Life of Biblical Texts* (Cambridge, MA: Harvard University Press, 1990).

27 Ibn Ishaq, *Life of Muhammad: A Translation of Ibn Ishaq's Sirat Rasul Allah*, ed. and trans. Alfred Guillaume (Oxford: Oxford University Press, 1955), 239.

28 Gordon D. Newby, *The Making of the Last Prophet: A Reconstruction of the Earliest Biography of Muhammad* (Columbia: University of South Carolina Press, 1989).

29 Newby, *The Making of the Last Prophet*, 3–4.

30 See Fred M. Donner, *Narratives of Islamic Origins: The Beginning of Islamic Historical Writings* (Princeton: Darwin Press, 1998), 147–156.

31 Ibn Ishaq, *Life of Muhammad*, 69.

32 Ibn Ishaq, *Life of Muhammad*, 79.

33 Ibn Ishaq, *Life of Muhammad*, 80.

34 Ibn Ishaq, *Life of Muhammad*, 246.
35 This section builds on my "Religion Without Religion: Integrating Islamic Origins into Religious Studies," *Journal of the American Academy of Religion* 85, no. 4 (2017): 867–888.
36 *Doctrina Iacoba* V.16 in Gilbert Dagron and Vincent Déroche, "Juifs et Chrétiens dans l'Orient du VIIe siècle," *Traveaux et mémoires* 11 (1991): 17–273, at 209–210.
37 Patricia Crone and Michael Cook, *Hagarism: The Making of the Islamic World* (Cambridge: Cambridge University Press, 1977), 4.
38 Stephen J. Shoemaker, *The Death of a Prophet: The End of Muhammad's Life and the Beginnings of Islam* (Philadelphia: University of Pennsylvania Press, 2012), 24.
39 On this text, see Moritz Steinschneider, "Apocalypsen mit polemischer Tendenz," *Zeitschrift der Deutschen Morgenlandischen Gesellschaft* 28 (1874): 627–659; a translation may be found in Bernard Lewis, "An Apocalyptic Vision of Islamic History," *Bulletin of the School of Oriental and African Studies* 13 (1950): 308–338. More generally, see Shoemaker, *The Death of a Prophet*, 28–31.
40 Crone and Cook, *Hagarism*, 4–5.
41 Steven M. Wasserstrom, *Between Muslim and Jew: The Problem of Symbiosis Under Early Islam* (Princeton: Princeton University Press, 1995), 181–205.
42 Lewis, "An Apocalyptic Vision of Islamic History," 313.
43 Shoemaker, *The Death of a Prophet*, 32.
44 Although the text, a major historical work in the Coptic Orthodox Church, was first compiled in late antiquity, it has been continually revised and updated over the centuries. In this regard, see David W. Johnson, "Further Remarks on the Arabic History of the Patriarchs of Alexandria," *Oriens Christianus* 61 (1977): 103–116. Originally written in Coptic, the text was translated into Arabic in the tenth century.
45 Qtd. in Shoemaker, *The Death of a Prophet*, 39–40.
46 Jaroslav Stetkevych, *Muhammad and the Golden Bough: Reconstructing Arabian Myth* (Bloomington: Indiana University Press, 1996), 1–12.
47 See, e.g., Muhammad Hamidullah, *The First Written Constitution in the World: An Important Document of the Time of the Holy Prophet*, 3d rev. ed. (Lahore: Sh. Muhammad Ashraf, [1394] 1975).
48 Michael Lecker, *The Constitution of Medina: Muḥammad's First Legal Document* (Princeton: Darwin Press, 2004), 77.

2 Growth

If the previous chapter presented what we know realistically about relations in the earliest years of Jewish-Muslim interaction, the present one turns to what is generally recognized to be their zenith. The relationship that developed between Muslims and Jews in the Middle Ages – especially in places like al-Andalus (Muslim Spain), Baghdad, and Cairo – is often held up as the so-called golden age of their mutual coexistence. While I certainly do not want to deny such coexistence here, I do think it important to note that a "golden age" is by definition a romantic or wistful slogan that is applied retroactively onto another time or place. Every age, accordingly, is a golden age to someone or some group. The result is that "golden ages" tend to tell us more about ourselves, including our own desires, than they do about anything we might label as historical.

Implicit in a golden age of Jewish-Muslim relations is the distinctly modern and irenic notion of tolerance, whether religious or otherwise. The past, however, has often been stripped of its actual historical contexts so that it can be held up as an antidote to the ills between the two groups, now often imagined as Israeli and Arabs or Palestinians, in the present. Places like Muslim Spain then become the inverse of the modern Middle East.[1]

Despite the fact that we begin to walk upon firmer terrain in the period covered in this chapter, we must be cautious of simply jumping from the murkiness of the last chapter to places like Muslim Spain. In between these two periods there reside many lacunae and blind spots. The period emerging after late antiquity, from roughly the death of Muhammad in 632 to the death of Saadya Gaon, one of the most important framers of rabbinic Judaism and someone who wrote primarily in Arabic, in 942, is among the most obscure in Jewish history. Basic questions include: What happened to the Jews on the Arabian Peninsula after the death of Muhammad? Were they simply folded into the burgeoning Muslim community (*umma*)? Did they leave to other places? Or, perhaps it was some combination of these two alternatives?[2]

While we may possess more texts than before, these texts rarely speak to or about the other. We have, for example, Jewish literary and legal texts, in addition, of course, to many Arabic ones. Only gradually, though, do they seem to have taken cognition of the other. As David Wasserstein has observed the fact remains that most Muslims barely noticed the literary and intellectual production of Jews.[3] In the words of Jacob Lassner, "at best the Jews are shadowy figures in the pages of the Muslim chronicles, geographical writings and belletristic texts."[4] When Jews make an appearance in Muslim texts the concern is less about real Jews than about fictive ones. Not infrequently Jews function as literary stand-ins for heterodox Muslims so that theoretical "Jews" are deployed to think about actual Muslim bodies and ideas.

Retaining the tenor of the previous chapter, the present one again seeks to show the creation of a textual boundary, on either side of which ideas or beliefs could be placed and simultaneously defined as "Jewish" or "Muslim." Again, though, these are often little more than literary conceits. For medieval Muslims, "the Jew," as mentioned, often functioned as a trope against which Sunni orthodoxy could be articulated and maintained. "Jews" and "Jewish" thus could be used as a code to designate the inverse or opposite of what was imagined to be normative belief. In this regard, it is not uncommon to find "Jew" used alongside the cognate *al-Rafida*, literally "rejectors," a generic term used to denote those who reject legitimate Islamic authority and leadership, and which Sunnis often used to refer to the Shia.[5] Indeed, according to such Sunni sources, even the founder of the Shia, Abd Allah ibn Saba, was a Jew.[6]

Yet, if "Jew" or "Judaism" in the hands of medieval Muslim texts becomes a way to think about heterodoxy, in medieval Jewish texts the locution "Islam" or "Muslim" has a rather different connotation. Such terms now function, perhaps not surprisingly given the fact that Jews were a minority within Islam, much more quietly and on a more subterranean level for correct praxis and belief. Islamic ideas and Muslim practices – as witnessed among theologians, philosophers, and mystics – are regarded as those to which Judaism ought to aspire. In this, we see parallels with German-Jewish thinkers in the nineteenth century who imagined German Protestantism, and all of the literary and cultural aspects associated with it, in a similar light.

For the sake of convenience the present chapter is subdivided into three sections that, for many, represent the florescence of Jewish-Muslim relations in the Middle Ages: theology, philosophy, and mysticism. Running as a leitmotif throughout this chapter is, once again, the figment of a firm line separating Jew and Muslim. Certainly this boundary is more stable than that encountered in the previous chapter. However, we still need to be aware that Muslim and Jewish thinkers tended to be more ambiguous about the ethnic and religious boundaries that we now employ in the modern period to describe them.

As in the previous chapter and in the following one, we also see this period as a source of anxiety for us in the present. This means that we tend to view the relations between Jews and Muslims in the medieval period as something they were not, nor indeed could have been. Terms like "tolerance," "interfaith," "convivencia," and the like do little more than make medieval Jews and Muslims into that which we want them to be in order to try to solve the unpleasantness of our present messy and contentious situation.

Before I continue a cautionary word is in order. Though my focus in this chapter, in keeping with the tenor of the volume, leans toward theology and philosophy, it is important to remember that philosophizing and theologizing are, for the most part, an elite activity. It is certainly not the best, let alone only, domain in which to explore Muslim-Jewish relations. Within this context, philosophical, theological, and mystical texts were produced in distinct social and literary contexts, and also studied in such contexts.[7] Reading, writing, and studying are not timeless activities, in other words, but occur in real and specific contexts.

Even more than this, we must not forget the daily lives and social interactions of the individuals who produced such texts as witnessed in treasure troves such as the Cairo Genizah ("storehouse" for worn-out Hebrew manuscripts or anything else with the divine name on it), so ably introduced to us through the pioneering work of Goitein.[8] The documents associated with this Genizah reveal, as numerous scholars since Goitein have demonstrated, the integration of Jewish life into an Islamic environment. In the words of Phillip I. Ackerman-Lieberman, quotidian social interactions "provided the Jewish community with a vehicle for expressing its own cultural distinctiveness . . . in the broader 'Islamic' marketplace."[9] While I might not draw as firm a line when it comes to "cultural distinctiveness," I would say that, in keeping with the theme of the present study, it was in the marketplace – just as it was in the seminary – that Muslim and Jew thought about, with, and from the other.

Theology (*Kalam*)[10]

The birth of theological speculation is, generally speaking, associated with religious controversy and the subsequent need to articulate and justify a set of beliefs and/or practices that will eventually become normative or orthodox. Although it is important not to reduce theological speculation to outside influence,[11] the most important impetus for the rise of rationalist theology in Islam was contact with Greek sources, especially those associated with logic, and the concomitant need to try and reconcile the terminology and categories of rationalism with those of monotheism. This attempt at reconciliation is known as *Kalam*, and its practitioners are known as *mutakallimun* (sg. *mutakallim*).

Kalam originated in Islamic circles before making inroads among Jewish thinkers. Most works of *Kalam*, whether Muslim or Jewish, share a similar style and structure. They usually take the form of theological *summae* to define correct belief and practice, beginning from universal principles (e.g., creation of the world, epistemology) before moving to more specific concerns (e.g., prophecy, the afterlife). The texts are usually polemical, providing the believer with responses to criticism of his or her religion (e.g., "if an unbeliever should say 'x,' one should respond to him with the claim that . . .").

Among the earliest practitioners of *Kalam* were the Mutazila, also referred to as *ahl al-adl wa'l-tawhid* (the people of [divine] justice and unity). In addition to stressing God's unity and justice – by which they meant that He could not do something that would contravene justice – they emphasized the importance of reason (*aql*) in religious speculation. One of the most important synthetic works describing the doctrine of the Mutazila may be found in Abd al-Jabbar's (d. 1025) *Al-mughni* ("Summa"), which emphasizes the importance of four sources for ascertaining truth: the Quran, agreed upon hadiths (sayings of Muhammad), rational argument, and *ijma* (i.e., consensus).[12]

The Mutazila developed a comprehensive theological framework that revolved around a number of key features: God's unity, God's justice, the intermediate state of the grave sinner (i.e., as neither an infidel nor pious Muslim), reward and punishment in the afterlife, and the ethical notion that one must avoid sin and practice virtue.[13] During the ninth and tenth centuries, the Mutazila enjoyed tremendous success, using their rationalist principles to develop an important and influential body of scientific and exegetical literature. Their two main epicenters were Basra and Baghdad, both of which had fairly large Jewish communities that would, as we shall see presently, absorb the general theological framework of the Mutazila.

The Mutazila would come under criticism from at least two constituencies. The first was the philosophers, who regarded *mutakallimun* as little more than apologists for their religion. The great philosopher Alfarabi (870–950), for example, has the following to say about *Kalam* in his *The Enumeration of the Sciences*:

> And still others, convinced of the validity of their own religion beyond any doubt, hold the opinion that they should defend it before others, show it to be fair and free it of suspicion, and ward off their adversaries from it, by using any chance thing. They would not even disdain to use falsehoods, sophistry, confounding, and contentiousness.[14]

Writing much later, the Jewish philosopher Maimonides (d. 1204) argued that such theologians "are of the opinion that what may be imagined is an admissible notion for the intellect."[15] Maimonides is here critical of those who argue for an arrangement of the universe that is arbitrary in order that they may protect God's omnipotence and omniscience. Such a view was diametrically opposed to the Aristotelian universe upon which the philosophers' natural science was predicated. According to these theologians, Maimonides further writes, "it should come about that the sphere of the earth should turn into a heaven endowed with a circular motion and that the heaven should turn into the sphere of the earth."[16]

The Mutazila, however, also came under attack by other schools of *Kalam*, which sought to rewrite the relationship between religion and reason. This seems to have been precipitated by the *mihna* ("inquisition") developed by the Caliph al-Mamun (d. 833), which consisted of a theological test, wherein religious scholars had to swear allegiance to the Mutazila doctrine that the Quran was created in time. Were it not created in time, they argued, the Quran would be coeval with God, thereby compromising God's singularity. Those theologians who refused to assent to this principle were jailed, leading Goldziher to remark, years ago, that we should avoid thinking of the Mutazila as the "free-thinkers" of early Islam.[17] One of the most important individuals who refused to swear to the doctrine of a created Quran was Ahmad ibn Hanbal (780–855), someone who would become one of the most esteemed doctrinal authorities in the Sunni tradition. For ibn Hanbal, Muslims had all that they needed in a literal reading of the Quran and hadith, and there was no need for a Greek (i.e., pagan) inflected rationalism to ascertain good from bad.

Following Ibn Hanbal's lead, another branch of *Kalam*, the Ashariyya, responded to what would in hindsight amount to the temporary ascendency of the Mutazila. They claimed, in general terms, that human reason was incapable of establishing truth claims with absolute certainty or confidence because God transcended the narrow parameters of human reason. Many associated with this theological school argued that if the Quran ascribes attributes to God, we must accept them "without asking how" (*bi-la kayf*). In the creedal statement of al-Ashari (d. 936), the founder of this school, we read, "God has a face, without asking how, as it says 'the face of your Lord endures, full of majesty and honor.'"[18] Or, again, believers "affirm hearing and sight of God, and do not deny that as do the Mutazila."[19]

It would, however, be a mistake to conceive of the Ashariyya simply as anti-rationalist. In this regard, they developed a highly technical and atomistic framework, wherein they argued that God constantly engages in the act of creation, meaning that God could, should He so desire, create a different world at any moment from the one we know. Such a position, needless to say, protects the absolute omnipotence of God, whereas the Mutazila – at least according to this position – sought to harness God's power by subsuming it under human rationalism. The Ashariyya also developed a technical description of human will that tried to combine human freedom (people are responsible for their actions) with determinism (to maintain God's omniscience and omnipotence). According to al-Ashari, the faithful "hold that a [person] has no acting-power to do anything before he [actually] does it, and that he is not able to escape God's knowledge or do a thing that God knows he will not do."[20]

The development of rational theology in Judaism took place, not surprisingly, in Arabic and under the general intellectual milieu produced by Islamic thinkers. Jewish theologians, then, defined Judaism in a manner that was theologically similar, if not actually identical, to what Muslim theologians did. As Jews adopted Arabic and as they began to think in Arabo-Islamic categories, it was only natural that they would begin to try and connect the themes of rationalist theology that they encountered among Arab-Muslim thinkers both to articulate and to interpret their own religious tradition. The result was the rise of what we may call, albeit somewhat problematically, Jewish *Kalam*, which was primarily of the Mutazila form.

Jewish *Kalam*, like that of the Muslim variety, begins with the premise that both the unaided human intellect and sense perception form the basic sources of knowledge. Human reason, in other words, is what enables the individual to make sense of the universe, to know, for example, that it is created *ex nihilo* by an omnipotent and omniscient Creator that is fundamentally or essentially different from His creation. Human reason is also the primary means and method with which to engage in the interpretation of the Bible.

Dawud al-Muqammis (d. ca. 937) is generally regarded as one of the earliest rationalists in Judaism. His place in the so-called canon of medieval Jewish rationalism, however, is complicated by, among other things, his purported conversion to Christianity (and subsequent reversion to Judaism).[21] Unlike other Jewish *mutakallimun*, al-Muqammis composed his major theological work – *Ishrun al-maqala*, or *The Twenty Chapters* – in Arabic as opposed to Judeo-Arabic (i.e., Arabic written in Hebrew characters). Even the biblical prooftexts were translated into Arabic and written in Arabic characters.

The work itself is based on many of the typical themes that other *mutakallimun* were interested in, such as the sources of knowledge, the world, God, revelation, and the refutation of other religions. In Chapter Seven of the work, for example, al-Muqammis, in typical fashion, argues that the created nature of the world necessarily implies the existence of a Creator:

> If someone asks, "How do we know that it is impossible for a thing to create itself?" We reply that had it created its own self, only two possibilities could have obtained at the time of its creation: either it created itself when it existed, or it created itself when it did not exist. If it created itself when it was already existing, it means that it existed before it created itself.[22]

Al-Muqammis continues by arguing that the world could neither have generated itself nor have been created from preexistent matter (*hayula*). Since createdness is an attribute of matter (*jawhar*), and not of the

Creator, he argues that this is proof that God, who possesses eternity as an essential attribute, created the world from nothing (*la min shay*). Perhaps on account of his conversion to Christianity and subsequent reversion to Judaism, he is particularly critical of his former religion, arguing that the claim that God is "one substance, but three hypostases" (*jawhar wahid thalatha aqanim*) goes against the dictates of reason. As we have just seen, al-Muqammis argues that to posit God as a substance (*jawhar*) is incompatible with His unity because substance implies the existence of created attributes, which God by definition cannot possess.

If Dawud al-Muqammiṣ represents the first generation of Jewish *mutakallimun*, Saadia Gaon (d. 942) represents the clearest example of the second generation.[23] Saadia was one of the rabbinic leaders (*geonim*; sg. *gaon*) associated with the academies of Sura and Pumbedita (both in Babylonia or modern day Iraq), and, as I have argued elsewhere, was largely responsible for the consolidation of rabbinic Judaism.[24] Since he spent considerable time in Baghdad, a hotbed of Mutazila speculation in the tenth century, his model for constructing rabbinic Judaism was the same type of rationalist Islam that Sunni *mutakallimun* were creating at the same time and in the same place. Saadia, for example, was among the first important rabbinic figures to write extensively in Arabic, and he is often considered to be one of the founders of Judeo-Arabic literature, composing works on linguistics, Jewish law (*halakha*), and theology, in addition to writing a Hebrew-Arabic dictionary known as the *Agron*. As a good *mutakallim*, he was also involved in religious polemics, seeking to articulate and defend rabbinic belief from the threat of the Karaites, a sectarian movement that denied the validity and authority of the Oral Torah.[25]

Saadia's most important work is his *Kitab al-amanat w'al-itiqadat*, "The Book of Articles of Faith and Doctrines of Dogma," translated into Hebrew by Judah Ibn Tibbon in the twelfth century as *Sefer Emunot ve-Deot*. This work represents the first systematic attempt to integrate Jewish texts with various components of Greek philosophy. It is a work that helped to shape much subsequent rabbinic thought and remains today at the heart of traditional Judaism, perhaps unsurprisingly. It proved to be much more theologically compatible with traditional Judaism than Aristotelianism or Neoplatonism, which many perceived to be based on "foreign" wisdom. In the introduction to the work, Saadia writes:

> Blessed be the Lord, the God of Israel, to whom the truth is known with absolute certainty; who confirms to men the certainty of the

truths which their souls experience – finding as they do through their souls their sense perceptions to be trustworthy; and knowing as they do through their souls their rational knowledge to be correct, thereby causing their errors to vanish, their doubts to be removed, their proofs to be clarified, and their arguments to be well grounded. Glory unto Him who is exalted above all attributes and praise.[26]

Here Saadia informs the reader that sound sense perception and sound reason are able to establish truth for humans. He then argues that the goal of his book is to explain why individuals in the search for truth go astray and how such errors "can be removed so that the object of their investigations may be fully attained."[27] The majority of these errors, according to him, emerge from the fact that many individuals fail to grasp the phenomenon of sense perception. Either they have an inadequate idea of the object in question or their observations are premature. He gives us the following analogy:

Take the case of a person who is looking for someone called Reuben ben Jacob. He may be in doubt whether he has found him for one of two reasons: either because his knowledge of Reuben is inadequate, since he never met him before and therefore does not know him, or else because seeing some other person he may wrongly assume him to be Reuben, taking the least line of resistance and neglecting to make proper inquiries. He has no claim to be forgiven since he takes things too easily and conducts his search carelessly. The result will be that his doubts will never be cleared up.[28]

Saadia informs us that the same applies to rational knowledge. Only now errors occur either when the individual in question is unfamiliar with the methods of demonstration, meaning that the individual may be unable to differentiate between a valid and an invalid proof, or when the individual may understand proper argumentation, but still refuse to complete the work of rational investigation on account of haste.

All of this sounds virtually identical to what we find in works of Mutazila *mutakallimun*. How, then, does Saadia differ from them? Primary is his use of biblical prooftexts instead of Quranic ones. For example, he cites Psalm 119:18 – "Open Thou mine eyes, that I may behold wondrous things out of Your Law" – as proof that the biblical text supports the type of rationalizing theology that Saadia is engaged in. Or, again, he invokes

Isaiah 48:17 – "I am the Lord your God, who teaches you for your profit, who leads you by the way that you should go" – as further proof that it is incumbent upon the Jew to engage in rational speculation, despite the fact that the Bible probably had something else in mind.

More importantly, however, Saadia argues that Jews possess one feature that no other people do, and he calls this "reliable tradition" (*al-habar al-sadiq*). Whereas all people share the three basic sources of knowledge – sense perception, reason, and inferential knowledge (e.g., where there is smoke, there is fire) – only Jews possess a fourth. This final source of knowledge is what differentiates Jews from non-Jews:

> We, the congregation of the believers in the unity of God, accept the truth of all the three sources of knowledge, and we add a fourth source, which we derive from the three proceeding ones, and which has become a root of knowledge for us, namely the root of the reliable tradition [*al-habar al-sadiq*]. For it is based on the knowledge of sense perception and the knowledge of reason.[29]

In a subsequent chapter of the treatise, Saadia divides the commandments in Judaism into "laws of reason" and "laws of revelation." The former are ascertainable by reason (e.g., "Thou shalt not kill"), whereas the latter consist of "matters regarding which reason passes no judgment" (e.g., how ordinary days differ from festival ones). Saadia also argues that although reason can ascertain why murder or theft is wrong, humans need revelation to set the terms of punishment, and so on.

Before turning our attention to subsequent developments in Muslim and Jewish theology, it is worth underscoring – and this is the main point that I want to make here – that contact with Muslim rationalism forever transformed the way in which Judaism was both approached and defined.

Much of the early centuries of rational theology in Islam and Judaism involved individuals, like those we have already encountered, articulating what they considered to be their respective tradition's theological principles. Within this context, it is often difficult to differentiate Jewish *mutakallimun*, such as al-Muqammis and Saadia, from their Muslim contemporaries. Indeed, all that seems to separate the one set from the other is the adjective in front of the activity they all engaged in – *Kalam*. Since the very terms "Muslim *Kalam*" and "Jewish *Kalam*" are modern terms, it is difficult to know how "Jewish" someone like Saadia regarded his thinking to be. A good example of this may be found in the theological writings of Ibn Hazm (d. 1064), a Muslim polymath from al-Andalus, who makes references to the writings of al-Muqammis and Saadia in order to criticize them.[30] The criticism is not so important here as is the fact that he was familiar with their writings, thereby offering us a clear insight into the fact that Jewish and Muslim *mutakallimun* did not neatly and simply bifurcate into, as so many of our textbooks tell us, religious adjectives.

Subsequent centuries, however, saw an increased differentiation between Jewish and Islamic theology, especially as the language of theological speculation in Judaism switched from Arabic to Hebrew. Yet, even in subsequent centuries, we still witness the filiations between Muslim and Jewish theology. Ibn Kammuna (d. 1284), for example, was, by all accounts, a Jew, though some have argued that he had converted to Islam.[31] Although a Jew, his writings make pious remarks about Muhammad. He also wrote a detailed commentary to Suhrawardi's *al-Talwihat* ("Intimations"), and glosses to his young contemporary Fakhr al-Din al-Razi's *al-Malim* ("Waymarks"), an important work of Islamic theology. Ibn Kammuna's commentary on Suhrawardi's texts, in addition to his correspondences with Qutb al-Din al-Shirazi and Nasir al-Din al-Tusi, played a major role in both the exposition and diffusion of Suhrawardi's *Ishraqi*, or "Eastern," philosophy in later Muslim thought. Indeed, so important is Ibn Kammuna to the understanding of Muslim theology of this period that several contemporary Iranian scholars have concentrated their efforts on Ibn Kammuna's philosophical writings and have edited several of his works, specifically his commentary on Suhrawardi's *Talwihat*.[32] Individuals such as Ibn Kammuna nicely blur the boundary between Jewish theology and Muslim theology in this period. How, for example, do we classify him? Is he a "Jewish" theologian or a "Muslim" one? Such religious adjectives, I would suggest, are our terms, and may be unhelpful, thereby betraying our own set of concerns.

Ibn Kammuna is also known as the author of *Tanqih al-abhat li-l-milal al-thalath* ("Examination of the Inquiries into the Three Faiths"), a work, written in Arabic, that examines Judaism, Christianity, and Islam from what he calls an objective point of view.[33] In his introduction, he writes that "I have not been swayed by mere personal inclination, nor have I ventured to show preference for one faith over the other, but have pursued the investigation of each faith to its fullest extent."[34] In his chapter on Islam, he again summarizes the theological teachings of Islam with little or no polemical intent. He writes, therein that

> The Muslims agree that Muhammad Ibn Abdallah Ibn Abd al-Muttalib is the Messenger of God and Seal of the Prophets; that he was sent to all mankind, that he abrogated all the previous religions, and that his religion will remain in force to the day of resurrection; that he called upon men to believe in God and His angels, messengers, and scriptures, and to believe that God is one, has no companion, none like or similar to Him, no mate or child, and that God is preexistent, living, all-knowing, almighty, willing, hearing, seeing, speaking; and that He sent the Torah through Moses, the Gospel through Jesus; that Muhammad, on behalf of God, announced that He commanded the performance of prayer, payment of Zakat, fasting during Ramadan, pilgrimage to the sanctuary of Mecca.[35]

Another example is David b. Joshua, the great grandson of Maimonides, who lived in Cairo during the late thirteenth and early fourteenth centuries. If and when Maimonides's descendants are discussed, it is usually his son Abraham, a well-known halakhist and someone who was very much inspired by the mystical trends of Islamic mysticism. However, in the realm of theology, it is Maimonides's great grandson who deserves attention. As the *nagid* of the Jewish community there, he wrote, as many of Maimonides's descendants did, Sufi-inspired interpretations of Judaism. Most notable is his *al-Murshid ila-l-tafarrud wa-l-murfid ila-l-tagarrud* ("The Guide to Loneliness and the Path to Detachment").[36] There are also indications found in the Cairo Genizah that he wrote commentaries on the writings of al-Hallaj and Ibn Arabi.

Philosophy and mysticism[37]

In medieval Islam and Judaism it is often difficult to separate neatly what constitutes mysticism and what constitutes philosophy.[38] This may well be on account of the fact that these two terms are ours as opposed to being for those whom we are too easily willing to label as "philosophers" or "mystics." Many philosophers, for example, were also astrologers, and many engaged in what we would today call mystical speculation. In the medieval period, the difficulty in taxonomy may very well have been the result of the term "Neoplatonism." The term is notoriously imprecise and anachronistic. It was originally coined in the nineteenth century and was used pejoratively to denote later commentators to Plato and Aristotle, none of whom were thought to be as original as the great masters. Indeed, it was assumed that the very genre of commentary was unoriginal. The result is that today we label as "Neoplatonic" thinkers who did not see themselves as such, and, because of this, we group them under the rubric "Neoplatonic" despite the fact that their thought may well have had very little in common.[39] While the term may well reveal something, it also conceals a great deal. Certainly the textual and literary dimensions of Neoplatonism are well-defined in, for example, the various recensions of Plotinus in Arabic and Hebrew translations, and its doctrinal contours are also well known (e.g., emanationist cosmogonies, metaphysical hierarchical categories, and the pathos of the soul's upward return).

Based on such texts and doctrines, we can perhaps identify a set of Muslim and Jewish thinkers – e.g., al-Kindi, Isaac Israeli, Ikhwan al-Safa, Ibn Gabirol, and Bar Hiyya – as "Neoplatonic." Despite the fact that all of these thinkers are today considered to be philosophers, they all exhibited traits that we could define as mystical. Of central importance here is the imagination or the imaginative faculty, often referred to by medieval Islamic and Jewish thinkers as the inner eye (Ar. *al-ayn al-batiniyya*; Heb. *ein ha-lev*).[40] Within this context, virtually all philosophers – even those belonging to the more rationalist Aristotelian system – acknowledged that if the imagination is properly conditioned and works in tandem with the intellect, it could facilitate and permit access to the divine world. Since the noetic function of the imagination is to give form or corporeality to that which exists without form or body, it is able to move simultaneously between the celestial and mundane worlds, translating each into the other.[41] Even though many philosophers were overtly critical of the imagination, it is no coincidence that the telos of many of their systems is often an elaborate discussion of the philosopher's journey into the divine, which is often described in terms of rich and highly visual imagery.[42]

Let me cite several examples. In his Commentary to Qohelet 7:3, Abraham ibn Ezra (d. 1167) divides, as was customary in Neoplatonic circles, the human soul into three: the lowest or vegetative soul (*ha-nefesh ha-somehet*), the intermediate animal soul (*ha-nefesh ha-behema*), and the highest or rational soul (referred to as either *ha-neshamah* or *ha-lev*).

Though he writes in Hebrew, it is worth noting that all of the categories and technical terms that he employs derive from Arabo-Islamic philosophical tradition. The function of the animal soul, in the latter tradition, is to act as an intermediary between the higher and lower souls, to interact with the sensual world through the five senses, and then to process the data associated with this. The animal soul is crucial since it can either fall victim to the passions of the body or be used in the service of the intellect. Through a combination of theoretical and practical wisdom, one is able to perfect oneself in such a manner as to achieve a union (Heb. *devequt*; Ar. *ittisal*) with the Active Intellect, the last of the celestial intellects, associated with the sphere of the moon. Since the heart exists within a corporeal body, it is unable to know the upper worlds without recourse to vision. It is at this juncture that the imagination, what he frequently calls the "eye of the heart" (*ein ha-lev*), which translates the Arabic *al-ayn al-batiniyya*, becomes important. It is this faculty that allows the individual to see visions of the upper world by giving corporeal form to incorporeal phenomena. As he writes in his poem *bedat el edebeqa*:

> By the life that You give to me, I cleave to Your Torah
> I expect my reward to be given from God.
> In his Garden of Eden my will indulges in luxuries
> But when I search for Him, he is my reviver.
> It is You that I see in my imagination (*ein ha-lev*) and later
> In Your Torah, You are majestic in your strength.
> By my comprehension of the precepts of the straight path
> I praise You – and You increase my splendor.
> If mountains and valleys cannot confine
> Your glory (*kavod*) – then how can my words.
> In You my soul seeks refuge.[43]

In this passage we see a stunning example of the intersection of philosophical, mystical, and literary features that is one of the hallmarks of medieval Neoplatonism. Mystical vision is here intimately connected to literary expression and intellectual cultivation. Yet, and this is the key to Neoplatonism, the telos or the goal of the system is not reducible to the intellect, but is *supra*-rational. This is why Neoplatonism, as a form of medieval rationalism, must also be regarded as intimately connected to the mystical quest.

Even the great Aristotelian philosophers – such as al-Farabi, Ibn Sina, and Maimonides (d. 1204) – used this conception of the imagination, and their respective systems culminate in a similar visual quest that is often described using the pietistic language of Sufism. Avicenna, for example, writes in his *Kitab al-Isharat wa'l-Tanbihat* ("The Book of Pointers and Reminders") of the importance of vision in the philosophical quest. He even uses the technical Sufi term *arif* ("knower," in the sense of being a possessor of *marifa* or *irfan*, i.e., "mystical gnosis") to denote the philosopher who must align his or her soul through music, poetry, and thoughtful worship. In a telling chapter from the ninth section of the fourth part of his *Kitab al-Isharat wa'l-Tanbihat*, one entitled *fi maqamat al-arifin*, "on the stations of the knowers," he writes:

> If the sense perceptions are reduced and fewer preoccupations remain, it is not unlikely for the soul to have escapes that lead from the work of the imagination to the side of sanctity. Thus, apprehensions of the invisible world are imprinted on the soul, which then flow to the word of the imagination and are then imprinted in the common sense.[44]

Maimonides, the individual who is generally considered to be the arch-rationalist of premodern Jewish thought, also picks up these themes. We see them at work, for example, in what is sometimes referred to as the "Sufi" chapter in his philosophical magnum opus, *The Guide of the Perplexed*. In this chapter, which some believe he originally intended to conclude his *Guide*,[45] Maimonides provides his famous parable of the palace.[46] Therein he writes:

> The ruler is in his palace, and all his subjects are partly within the city and partly outside the city. Of those who are within the city, some have turned their backs upon the ruler's habitation, their faces being turned another way. Others seek to reach the ruler's habitation, turn toward it, and desire to enter it and to stand before him, but up to now they have not yet seen the wall of the habitation. Some of those who seek to reach it have come up to the habitation and walk around it searching for its gate. Some of them have entered the gate and walk about it in the antechambers. Some of them have entered the inner court of the habitation and have come to be with the king, in one and the same place as him, namely, in the ruler's habitation.

But their having come into the inner part of the habitation, it is indispensable that they should make another effort; then they will be in the presence of the ruler, see him from afar or nearby, or hear the ruler's speech or speak to him.[47]

It should be clear that, in invoking Sufi terminology and images, Maimonides is not suggesting to his Jewish readers that they become Muslims or Sufis. On the contrary, what he is doing is importing Sufic terminology and categories in order to push elite Jews like himself to a deeper understanding of the commandments and, through them, of God. This deeper understanding, however, comes only from an understanding that is imported from the Islamic mystical tradition. So while Maimonides does not want his followers to become Muslims, he does want them to be like Sufis, whose understanding of Islam, he maintains, is correct.

Islamic terms and Jewish critics

Even those Jewish thinkers critical of the intersection between Judaism and Islam were ultimately forced to use technical Arabo-Islamic terms to defend and subsequently to define Judaism. Judah Halevi (1075–1141) represents, on one level, a quintessential Jewish thinker from Muslim Spain.[48] Secular and religious poet, philosopher, and rabbi, he is perhaps best known for writing one of the most articulate pleas for Jewish particularity and chosenness. His *Kitab al-radd wa'l-dalil fi'l-din al-dhalil*, "The Book of Refutation and Proof in Defense of the Despised Religion," also known as the *Kitab al-khazari*, was, as should be clear from its title, written in Arabic.[49] Note the paradox that a plea for the uniqueness of the Jewish people would be written in Arabic as opposed to Hebrew, especially when we know that Halevi wrote also in Hebrew. Significantly, Halevi wrote the book in the form of a dialogue, a genre largely unused in earlier Jewish thought, but one that was common among Muslim esoteric groups such as the Ismailis.[50]

In an important study from the 1980s, the Israeli intellectual historian Shlomo Pines demonstrated how Halevi adopted and adapted several terms from the Ismailis. One such term is *safwa*, which the Ismailis used to denote an elite line of prophets.[51] Halevi, however, uses this term not to refer to a line of prophets, but to the entire Jewish people. In *Khuzari* I: 44–47, the haver, the main protagonist and the representative of normative Judaism, informs the proselyte, who has just asked him what the date is:

> Four thousand and nine hundred years. The details can be demonstrated from the lives of Adam, Seth, Enoch to Noah, then Shem and Eber to Abraham, then Isaac and Jacob to Moses. These [individuals] possess a connection [*ittisalahum*] to Adam on account of his election [*safwa*]. Each of them had children who were like empty vessels when compared to their fathers because the divine influence did not unite with them [*lam yittasalu bi-hum amr ilahi*]. This account occurs through sainted persons [*al-ilahun*] who were individuals and not a group until Jacob gave birth to the twelve tribes who all united with the divine influence [*kullahum yasilun li-l-amr al-ilahi*].[52]

All of Israel, according to Halevi here share in and inherit the divine influence (*amr ilahi*) on account of their descent from their ancestors. In like manner, Halevi takes the technical terms *amal/niyya*, which the Ismailis had used to elevate the former term at the expense of the latter, and inverts them. According to him religious actions – inscribed on and by the body – are as important, if not more so, as spiritual intention. In the dramatic opening to the Khuzari, an angel appears to the king in his dream and informs him:

> "Your intention [*niyya*; pl. *niyyat*] is pleasing to God, but your action [*amal*; pl. *amal*] is not." Yet he was so zealous in the cult of the Khazar religion, and with a pure and sincere *niyya* he devoted himself to the *amal* of the temple and the offering of sacrifices. Yet the angel came again at night and said to him: "Your *niyya* is pleasing, but your *amal* is not."[53]

Halevi's use of these two technical terms is the exact opposite of that found in Ismaili texts. In these latter texts, the *amal* are meant for all Muslims, but only a select few properly understand the *niyyat* behind them.

What Halevi has done, then, is taken an Ismaili genre (e.g., the dialogue), Ismaili terminology, and a similar narrative structure (one wherein a potential disciple asks a potential teacher for help), but giving them a radically different interpretation. In so doing, Halevi defines Judaism using Islamic concepts and terms of reference, even if by negating them.

That he uses such terms and genres shows how Islam structures his understanding of Judaism. The result is, once again, a Judaism whose essence is by no means fixed, and the terminology used to bring it into existence or at the very least give it definition is Islamic, and, again, not just Arabic.

"Jewish Sufism"

We see something similar at work in texts written by so-called Jewish Sufis. Though the term itself is somewhat problematic, it is not entirely inaccurate. What such terms try to convey is that certain Jews were attracted to certain teachings of certain Sufis – that is, Muslim mystics – and that they tried to adopt and adapt these teachings into a Jewish religious environment. While certainly there would have been contact between them, pietistic Jews inspired by Sufism were not actively telling their disciples they had to be Sufis, only that they should be more pietistic like them.

Since Maimonides saw the telos of the intellectual quest to be a quasimystical apprehension of the divine presence, it is perhaps no coincidence that his descendants were among the most articulate expositors on this intersection between Judaism and Islamic mysticism. Before I examine them, however, allow me to look briefly at the writings of Bahya ibn Paquda (b. 1050), a Jew, whose *Kitab al-Hidaya ila Faraid al-Qulub* ("The Book of Directions to the Duties of the Heart") represents one of the earliest attempts to introduce Sufi terminology into Judaism. However, there is little evidence that the work gave rise to a brand of Jewish pietists, as say the work of Abraham or Obadyah Maimonides would.[54]

Bahya, as Diana Lobel has shown, was a very synthetic thinker.[55] For example, he absorbed many of the premises of *Kalam*, such as arguments for the creation of this world out of nothing, in addition to adopting its basic method of argumentation. Bahya is customarily identified as a "Jewish philosopher" in the sense that he employs philosophical arguments to clarify religious belief by eradicating misconceptions about God and the divine world, and philosophy also serves as a reminder to the pious one when he or she becomes distracted by the needs of the body. However, for Bahya, philosophy and theology are but initial steps on the mystical path, a path that he describes in the introduction to his magnum opus as ascertaining the duties of the body and those of the heart. Whereas the former are external and concern the body, the latter are internal and involve "secret duties." In the introduction to the work, Bahya writes:

> Thus I have come to know for certain that the duties of the members are of no avail to us unless our hearts choose to do them and our soul desires their performance. Since, then our members cannot perform an act unless our souls have chosen it first, our members could free themselves from all duties and obligations if it should occur to us that our hearts were not obliged to choose obedience to God. Since it is clear that our Creator commanded the members to perform their duties, it is improbable that He overlooked our hearts and souls, our noblest parts, and did not command them to share in His worship, for they constitute the crown of obedience and the very perfection of worship.[56]

Bodily actions, in other words are meaningless unless they are informed by the proper duties of the heart. It is only the latter, according to Bahya, that make the former possible. Despite this, and here he foreshadows the comments in both Maimonides and his descendants, the most Jews only perform their religion externally. True worship (Ar. *ibada*; Heb. *avoda*), according to Bahya, involves a wholehearted devotion (*al-ikhlas*) to God, something that can occur only when the individual has purified oneself from spiritual blemish. The Sufi overtones of such a claim should be apparent, and indeed *ikhlas* is a technical term (in addition to being a chapter of the Quran) that Bahya has again introduced into Judaism. Indeed, the book translated into Hebrew by Judah Ibn Tibbon as *Hobot ha-Lebabot* would go on to become a timeless work of Jewish pietism, especially in Eastern Europe in subsequent centuries.

Like many Sufi manuals, Bahya's work is divided into gates, each of which describes a particular state or awareness that the seeker needs to embody. Bahya does not, however, present the various stages that the mystic must go through in the way that systematic Muslim Sufis like al-Qushayri (986–1074) do. This may well be on account of the fact that Bahya presents an intellectual journey as much as a spiritual one, and in fact does not see, as was typical in medieval Neoplatonism, the two modes as unconnected from one another. In the final gate, that of the true love (*sidq fi 'l-mahabba*) of God, Bahya articulates those who truly love God. This description, as Georges Vajda has shown, has parallels in

Muslim mystic Abu Nuaym al-Isfahani's *Hilyat al-Awliya* ("The Adorn-
ment of the Saints").[57] Bahya subsequently argues that the ultimate state
of love culminates in reliance (*tawakkul*) on the divine. In part seven of
the final gate, he writes:

> This way of worship is included in the duties of the heart. This is
> the inner knowledge (*ilm al-batin*) hidden in the hearts of those who
> know and contained in their inner being. When they speak of it, its
> truth becomes apparent to all, for every person of sound mind and
> intelligence will attest to its truthfulness and justice. This is the way
> they attain to the highest stage of God's obedience and reach the
> noblest rank of devotion [*ikhlas*] to God and truthfulness in love
> of him [*sidq fi 'l-mahabba*] in heart and soul, body and property, as
> stressed by the prophet, "And you shall love the Lord your God with
> all your heart, soul, and might." Those who have reached this stage
> are closest to the rank of the virtuous prophets [*al-anbiya al-abrar*]
> and God's chosen favorites [*al-asfiya al-akhyar*]. The Scriptures
> describe them as "lovers of God" and "lovers of His name," and it is
> said "That I may cause those that love me to inherit substance, and
> that I may fill their treasuries."[58]

Although Bahya certainly carries on the intellectual program of the
Neoplatonists as encountered in the previous section, it is also safe to say
that his use of Sufi terminology and categories is much more sustained
and systematic than anything found in these other thinkers.

Maimonides's son Abraham (1186–1237) succeeded his father as
the *nagid* of the Jewish community of Egypt, which meant that he was
the highest legal authority in the region. He was also an accomplished
physician, philosopher, and halakhist. In addition to all of this, he was
fascinated with the Sufis and their pietistic expressions, and he sought
to bring some of their teachings into Judaism.[59] Abraham seems to have
also admired the Islamic mystics; he called them the direct descendants
of the prophets, and regretted that his contemporary Jews did not follow
their example.[60] To try and rectify this he took many of their practices and
surrounded himself with disciples with the aim of creating a path (*tariqa*)
toward spiritual perfection. Like many Sufis, his enemies criticized him
for holding heretical beliefs and doctrines. For Abraham, however, the
path to God, and here he invokes the technical discussion of Sufi stations (*maqamat*), involved mercy, gentleness, humility, trust in God,

contentedness, abstinence, gentleness, fighting against one's nature, the control of faculties to serve spiritual ends, and solitude.[61] Travel in and through these stations must take place, according to him, by means of the scrupulous fulfillment of the law.

In his *Kifayat al-Abidin* ("The Guide for the Pious"), Abraham Maimonides distinguishes between two types of fulfilling the law: a mundane way and a special way. He differentiates them as follows:

> As for the common way it is a way of [consisting] in the performance of the explicit commandments – i.e., the carrying out of what is commanded to be done and the avoidance of what is commanded not to be done – by every person in Israel according to his requirements thereof . . . as for the special way it is the way [that takes account] of the purposes of the commandments and their secrets and of what can be understood of the intentions of the Law and the lives of the prophets and the saints and their ilk . . . the best name for him is a *hasid* because it is derived from *hesed*, the meaning of which is benevolence for he goes beyond what is required of him according to the explicit sense of the Law.[62]

Here, Abraham distinguishes between two ways to fulfill the commandments. In a distinction that goes back in Jewish pietism at least to Bahya, but in Sufism back much earlier, he argues that those who go over and above the simple performance of religious obligations are the true people of faith. But it is a path that is open only to the initiated: "The reason we say it is a special way is because it is not explicitly obligatory, and therefore no secular punishment by human hands applies to him who is remiss in it."[63] The *hasid*, then, is the one who engages in supererogatory acts of faith and is someone, to use the language of Sufism, who tries to understand the *tariqa* ("order" or "path") behind the *sharia* (the "law"), or the *batin* ("esoteric") behind the *zahir* ("exoteric").

This movement from the revealed to concealed and from the manifest to the hidden represents the essence of Sufism and the teachings of those Jews who sought to introduce it into Jewish thought and practice. It was not, to reiterate, the adoption of Islam at the expense of Judaism; it was, on the contrary, the adaptation of a certain mystically inspired language to mine the deeper truths of Judaism. We see this at work in Abraham's son Obadyah Maimonides and his *al-Maqala al-Hawdiyya* ("Treatise of the Pool"). In this treatise, we see again the uses to which the language and categories of the Islamic mystical tradition were put not only in the family of Maimonides, but in a certain elite cross-section of the Jewish community of Cairo. Obadyah, like his father and like other Jewish pietists, is extremely critical of what passes for contemporary belief. He writes, for example, that

> It has been repeatedly said that true devotion (*al-ibada al-haqiqiyya*) stems from the heart. As it is said, "And to serve Him with all your heart and all your soul" (Dt. 11:13). This is indeed the goal of the exoteric law. If an individual turns toward Him, it needs to be with the totality of his heart. Few, however, accomplish such a thing, whether it be in prayer or in studying and listening to the reading of the Torah. Indeed, they occupy themselves with serving that which distracts them from proper worship and with knowing that which distracts them from this knowledge. Even the sole concern of those renowned for their science is to hear the interpretation of a biblical verse or a pleasant expression, such as a line of poetry, with which they can embellish their prayers, in short, something that will charm their listeners.[64]

We again witness the intersection of Sufi-inspired language, the medieval Neoplatonic tradition to which Obadyah was an heir, and a deep-seated criticism of contemporary Jewish practice, combined with a deep admiration for a particular strain of Islam. Many of these Jewish pietists were critical of prevailing forms of religious worship that, as we have already seen, they considered to be too exoteric and too focused on the body at the expense of the heart. As a result, they sought to create new forms of worship that they borrowed from the Sufis, but that they often claimed had previously existed in Judaism.

The fifth and final Maimonidean *nagid* of the Jewish community in Egypt was David ben Joshua Maimonides (d. 1415).[65] Like his predecessors, he was greatly influenced by Sufism. Like other Jews influenced by Sufi ideas, he translated Arabic technical terms designating mystics with the more autochthonous sounding *ḥasid*, and in passages lifted directly from Sufi manuals he replaced Quranic verses with biblical ones. This presumably had the effect of making his ideas seem less radical to a Jewish readership. The very title of his *al-Murshid ila al-Tafarrud* ("The Guide to Detachment"), for example, clearly reveals his Sufi sympathies. Fenton notes that each stage of the spiritual journey equates with a station (*maqam*) on the Sufi path.[66] Fenton also notes that numerous extracts of *Kalimat al-Tasawwuf* ("Sayings of Sufism") by Shihab al-Din Suhrawardi (d. 1191) are found in this treatise.

Again, we witness elite Jewish thinkers using Islam – or at least a certain and equally elite version of it – as their model. In so doing, they create Judaism in Islam's image.

Shabbetai Zvi and the Dönmeh

The influence of Islamic mysticism on Jewish thought was not confined to al-Andalus and the western Mediterranean basin, however. After the expulsion from Spain in 1492, the development of Jewish mysticism took place virtually exclusively in Islamic lands. Despite this, there has not been nearly enough research devoted to the possible influence of Islamic mystical ideas and practices on Jewish mysticism and vice versa. The pioneering scholar of Jewish mysticism, Gershom Scholem, for example, largely downplayed the relationship between Lurianic Kabbalah and Sufis.[67] In recent years, however, Paul Fenton has encouraged us to rethink this thesis,[68] and has demonstrated how Safed, the epicenter of Lurianic Kabbalah in the fifteenth century, was also an important place of Islamic mysticism and the home to a number of Sufi masters.[69] There was even a *zawiya* (Sufi lodge) there, and Fenton goes so far as to suggest that certain ritual activities in Lurianic Kabbalah, such as the visitation to saints' tombs and silent contemplation (Heb. *hitbodedut*; Ar. *khalwa*), were influenced by the similar rituals practiced among Sufis in the area.[70] Such visits were meant to help the mystic both to commune with the soul of the deceased saint and to visualize him or her. Further study of the interaction between Sufism and Kabbalah will undoubtedly reveal the mutual influences between these two traditions in general and specific individuals in particular.

One such individual is one of the most controversial figures in later Lurianic mysticism – the self-declared Messiah, Shabbetai Zvi (d. 1676). This individual spent some of his formative years in Salonika (today northeastern Greece), a city that was renowned for its Sufis, the majority of whom were Mevlevis, the school associated with Jalal al-Din Rumi, in addition to being a major center of Kabbalah and of rabbinic scholarship. After the rabbis of the city banished Shabbetai from Salonika he moved around the eastern Mediterranean before he finally ended up in Constantinople in 1666. Although he claimed to be the Messiah, he was arrested there and given the option of death or conversion to Islam. It seems that before he converted to Islam and even afterward he was familiar with Sufi theosophy, some of which he adopted and adapted into his teachings. He and his followers, for example, adopted 18 commandments – the number 18, as Baer notes, was a significant number for both Jews and Mevlevi Sufis – and he told his followers to "be scrupulous in their observance of some of the precepts of the Muslims," which included going on the *hajj* (pilgrimage to Mecca) and fasting during the month of Ramadan.[71] Shabbetai also seems to have befriended a number of well-known Sufis in the region of Constantinople, most notably Muhammad al-Niyazi (b. 1617).[72]

After Shabbetai Zvi converted to Islam, his not insignificant followers – from as far away as Yemen in the South and Amsterdam in the North – had three options. The majority realized that he was not the Messiah and returned to their previous lives and professions, where they now presumably practiced normative Judaism. Another group remained Jews but still referred to him as the Messiah. These individuals became known as Sabbateans. And a small number converted to Islam along with their Messiah. These individuals became known as the Dönmeh, a group that was externally Muslim, but internally Jewish. These "crypto-Jews," while presumably having nothing to do with normative Jews, remained open to Muslim influence, especially that of Sufism.[73] The Dönmeh practiced endogamy, had their own cemeteries, and developed a religion that thrived on secrecy. Using the Sufi notion of *taqiyya* ("pious dissimulation"), the Dönmeh cultivated secret initiation, rites, and rituals that permitted them to have their own inner religious life while appearing to be orthodox Muslims to the outside world.

Conclusions

This chapter has presented some of the key areas where we see, if not an actual crosspollination of ideas, then at the very least the absorption of Arabo-Islamic on the part of Jewish intellectuals. This was not just an absorption wherein Judaism stayed the same at its perceived core, but only adopted Islamic and Sufi teachings to its surface. Instead of such a mode I here wish to suggest that the encounter with Islam in the Middle Ages radically and forever altered Judaism. In order to account for this one-way traffic of ideas, a generation of earlier Jewish thinkers proclaimed that this represents the second half of the symbiotic relationship between Jews and Muslims. In the first part Jews were imagined to function as Islam's midwife; in the second installment, Jews (re)absorb or (re)take from Muslims certain literary genres that they subsequently use to articulate Judaism.

Yet, just as we witnessed in the previous chapter the problems inherent to the first half of this narrative, we must now admit that similar problems beset the second half. So, the present chapter has argued that when Muslims tended to think about Jews they did so in such a manner that they were thinking less about actual Jews and more about what were imagined as heterodox Muslims. "Jews" and "Jewish ideas" thus tended to function as a code for other Muslims. The result is that, as Wasserstein noted earlier, Muslims were but rarely interested in actual Jews or Jewish texts.

The situation with Jews was somewhat different. This difference would seem to stem from the fact that Jews were but one religious minority in a large, multiethnic empire. The Muslims in which Jews were interested were real Muslims, but largely those intellectuals who were at the forefront of defining Islam along theological, mystical, and philosophical lines. As I tried to argue, Jews were not only attracted to the ideas they encountered among such individuals, they actively created Judaism in Islam's image. This was not so much a borrowing as it was a full-scale redefinition of Judaism – and what Judaism should be – using Islam as the paradigm.

This interaction would run from roughly the ninth century to the nineteenth. It is at this point that we confront the third theme of this study, resentment.

Notes

1 On the White House lawn, former US President Bill Clinton could remark:

> Let us resolve that this new mutual recognition will be a continuing process in which the parties transform the very way they see and understand each other. Let the skeptics of this peace recall what once existed among these people. There was a time when the traffic of ideas and commerce and pilgrims flowed uninterrupted among the cities of the Fertile Crescent. In Spain and the Middle East, Muslims and Jews once worked together to write brilliant chapters in the history of literature and science. All of this can come to pass again.

The transcript of the speech may be found at http://millercenter.org/scripps/archive/speeches/detail/3925.

2 The following three paragraphs rework Hughes, *Shared Identities*, 127–129.

3 David J. Wasserstein, "The Muslims and the Golden Age of Jews in al-Andalus," *Israel Oriental Studies* 17 (1997): 109–125.

4 Jacob Lassner, "Genizah Studies in the United States: Its Past and Its Future Links to Near Eastern Historiography," in *A Mediterranean Society By S. D. Goitein: An Abridgement in One Volume* (Berkeley: University of California Press, 1999), 478.

5 Etan Kohlberg, "The Term 'Rāfida' in Imāmī Shī'ī Usage," *Journal of the American Oriental Society* 99, no. 4 (1979): 677–679. See also my *Shared Identities*, 126–130.

6 On the legend of Ibn Sabā', see Israel Friedlander, "Abdallah b. Saba, der Begründer der Shi'a, und sein jüdischer Ursprung," *Zeitschrift für Assyriologie* 23 (1909): 296–327 and 24 (1910): 1–46. See also Maria Massi Dakake, *The Charismatic Community: Shi'ite Identity in Early Islam* (Albany: State University of New York Press, 2007), 262; William Frederick Tucker, *Mahdis and Millenarians: Shī'ite Extremists in Early Muslim Iraq* (Cambridge: Cambridge University Press, 2008), 10–12.

7 See *Medieval Jewish Philosophy and Its Literary Forms*, eds. Aaron W. Hughes and James T. Robinson (Bloomington: Indiana University Press, 2019).

8 Shlomo Dov Goitein, *A Mediterranean Society: The Jewish Communities of the Arab World as Portrayed in the Documents of the Cairo Geniza*, 6 vols. (Berkeley: University of California Press, 1967–93).

9 Phillip I. Ackerman-Lieberman, *The Business of Identity: Jews, Muslims, and Economic Life in Medieval Egypt* (Stanford: Stanford University Press, 2013), 3.

10 This section reworks my "Theology: The Articulation of Orthodoxy," in *The Routledge Handbook of Muslim-Jewish Relations*, ed. Josef Meri (London and New York: Routledge, 2016), 77–94.

11 This influence, as we shall see shortly, is usually Greek or even Syriac. On the latter see Michael Cook, "The Origins of the *Kalām*," *Bulletin of the School of Oriental and African Studies* 43 (1980): 32–43.

12 Abd al-Jabbar, *A Critique of Christian Origins*, ed., trans., and ann. Gabriel Said Reynolds and Samir Khalil Samir (Provo: Brigham Young University Press, 2010).

13 See the exhaustive study in Michael Cook, *Commanding Right and Forbidding Wrong in Islamic Thought* (Cambridge: Cambridge University Press, 2010), 32–45.

14 Alfarabi, "The Enumeration of the Religious Sciences." in *Medieval Political Philosophy*, eds. Ralph Lerner and Muhsin Mahdi (Ithaca: Cornell University Press, 1963), 30.

15 Moses Maimonides, *The Guide of the Perplexed*, 2 vols., trans. with intro. Shlomo Pines (Chicago: University of Chicago Press, 1963), 206.

16 Maimonides, *Guide*, 206.

17 Ignaz Goldziher, *Introduction to Islamic Theology and Law*, trans. Andras and Ruth Hamori (Princeton: Princeton University Press, 1981), 101.

18 Qtd. in W. Montgomery Watt, *Islamic Creeds: A Selection* (Edinburgh: Edinburgh University Press, 1994), 41.

19 Qtd. in Watt, *Islamic Creeds*, 42.

20 Qtd. in Watt, *Islamic Creeds*, 42.
21 On his biography, see Sarah Stroumsa, *Dāwūd Ibn Marwān al-Muqammiṣ's Twenty Chapters ('Ishrun al-Maqāla)* (Leiden: Brill, 1989), 15–23. See also Shlomo Pines, "Jewish Christians of the Early Centuries of Christianity According to a New Source," *Proceedings of the Israel Academy of Sciences and Humanities* I, no. 13 (1966): 1–73, at 47–48.
22 Stroumsa, *Dāwūd Ibn Marwān al-Muqammiṣ's Twenty Chapters*, 126–127.
23 Although Judah ben Barzillai, a twelfth-century Catalan Talmudist, reports that Saadia actually studied with al-Muqammiṣ, there is no independent evidence that he did.
24 Hughes, *Shared Identities*, 82–103.
25 See the comments in Daniel Frank, *Search Scripture Well: Karaite Exegesis and the Origins of the Jewish Bible Commentary in the Islamic East* (Leiden: Brill, 2004), 248–257.
26 Saadia Gaon, "The Book of Doctrines and Beliefs," in *Three Jewish Philosophers*, trans. Alexander Altmann, 3rd ed. (London: The Toby Press, 2006), 141–142.
27 Saadia, *The Book of Doctrines and Beliefs*, 142.
28 Saadia, *The Book of Doctrines and Beliefs*, 142–143.
29 Saadia, *The Book of Doctrines and Beliefs*, 155.
30 For further information on Ibn Ḥazm, see Camilla Adang, *Muslim Writers on Judaism and the Hebrew Bible: From Ibn Rabban to Ibn Hazm* (Leiden: Brill, 1996), 59–69.
31 On the evidence, see Reza Pourjavady and Sabine Schmidtke, *A Jewish Philosopher of Baghdad: 'Izz al-Dawla Ibn Kammūna (d. 683/1284) and His Writings* (Leiden: Brill, 2009), 8–23.
32 See, e.g., Hossein Ziai and Ahmed Alwishah, eds., *Ibn Kammūna: Al-Tanqīḥāt fī sharḥ al-talwīḥāt. Refinement and Commentary on Suhrawardī's Intimations. A Thirteenth Century Text on Natural Philosophy and Psychology* (Costa Mesa: Mazda Publishers, 2003).
33 An English translation may be found in *Ibn Kammūna's Examination of the Three Faiths: A Thirteenth-Century Essay in the Comparative Study of Religion*, trans. Moshe Perlmann (Berkeley: University of California Press, 1971).
34 Perlmann, *Ibn Kammūna's Examination of the Three Faiths*, 1.
35 Perlmann, *Ibn Kammūna's Examination of the Three Faiths*, 67. This sounds very similar to the speech of the Christian that may be found in the opening paragraphs of Judah Halevi's *Kuzari*.
36 *Al-Murshid ilā-l-tafarrud wa-l-murfid ilā-l-tagarrud*, ed. and trans. into Hebrew by Paul B. Fenton (Jerusalem: Meqize Nirdamim, 1985).
37 This section reworks my "Mysticism: The Quest for Transcendence," in *The Routledge Handbook of Muslim-Jewish Relations*, ed. Josef Meri (London and New York: Routledge, 2016), 219–234
38 See, e.g., the classic work by Georges Vajda, *L'Amour de Dieu dans la théologie juive du Moyen Âge* (Paris: J. Vrin, 1957).
39 On the history of this term, see Maria Luisa Gatti, "Plotinus: The Platonic Tradition and the Foundation of Neoplatonism," in *The Cambridge Companion to Plotinus*, ed. Lloyd P. Gerson (Cambridge: Cambridge University Press, 1996), 22–27.

62   *Growth*

40 See Elliot R. Wolfson, *Through a Speculum that Shines: Vision and Imagination in Medieval Jewish Mysticism* (Princeton: Princeton University Press, 1997); also Aaron W. Hughes, *Texture of the Divine: Imagination in Medieval Islamic and Jewish Thought* (Bloomington: Indiana University Press, 2004), 82–114.
41 Henry Corbin called this the *mundus imaginalis*. See, e.g., Henry Corbin, *Creative Imagination in the Sufism of Ibn Arabi*, trans. Ralph Manheim (Princeton: Princeton University Press, 1969); idem, *Avicenna and the Visionary Recital* (Princeton: Princeton University Press, 1960).
42 This, perhaps, explains why Plato and Aristotle were so mistrustful of the imagination. See, in this regard, Richard Kearney, *The Wake of the Imagination: Ideas of Creativity in Western Culture* (London: Hutchinson, 1988), 30–35; Eva T. H. Brann, *The World of the Imagination: Sum and Substance* (Lanham: Rowman and Littlefield, 1991), 35–45.
43 *Religious Poems of Ibn Ezra*, ed. Israel Levin (Jerusalem: Israel Academy of Sciences and Humanities, 1975), vol. 1, p. 26.
44 Avicenna, *Kitāb al-Ishārāt wa'l-Tanbihāt*, vol. 3, ed. S. Dunya (Cairo: Dār al-Ma'ārif bi-Miṣr, 1960), 246–247. See further M. 'A. Khan, "Kitabu Ta'bi-ir-ruya of Abu 'Ali b. Sina," *Indo-Iranica* 9, no. 4 (1956): 43–77, at 44.
45 See, e.g., Shlomo Pines, "Maimonides' Halakhic Works and the *Guide of the Perplexed*," in *Maimonides and Philosophy*, eds. S. Pines and Y. Yovel (Dordrecht: Martinus Nijhoff, 1986), 9–11.
46 Maimonides, *The Guide of the Perplexed*, 2 vols., III. 51 (vol. 2, 618–628).
47 *Guide* III.51 (618).
48 Requisite biographical material may be found in Goitein, *A Mediterranean Society*, 5: 448–468; Hayyim Schirmann, "The Life of Judah Halevi," (in Hebrew) *Tarbiz* 9 (1937–1939): 35–54, 219–240, 284–305; 10 (1938–1939): 237–239; 11 (1939–1940): 125.
49 Judah Halevi, *Kitāb al-radd wa'l-dalīl fī'l-dīn al-dhalīl* (al-kitāb al-khazarī), ed. David H. Baneth and Haggai Ben-Shammai (Jerusalem: Magnes Press, 1977); a rather poor English translation may be found in *The Kuzari: An Argument for the Faith of Israel*, trans. Hartwig Hirschfeld (New York: Schocken, 1964). A much better French translation is in *Le Kuzari: Apologie de la religion méprisée*, trans. Charles Touati (Paris: Verdier, 1994).
50 See my *The Art of Dialogue in Jewish Philosophy* (Bloomington: Indiana University Press, 2008), 26–49. I refer the interested reader to this work. My reasons for including this material in the present context are much less technical: to show how Halevi's understanding of Judaism draws its inspiration from a Muslim subculture.
51 Shlomo Pines, "Shi'ite Terms and Conceptions in Judah Halevi's *Kuzari*," *Jerusalem Studies in Arabic and Islam* 2 (1980): 165–225, at 167–170.
52 *Kuzari* 1:44–47 (Hirschfeld, 49); see also 2:56 (Hirschfeld, 117).
53 *Kuzari* 1:1 (Hirschfeld, 35).
54 See Paul Fenton's introductory comments to Obadyāh Maimonides, *The Treatise of the Pool*, trans. P. Fenton (London: Octagon Press, 1981), 3.
55 Diana Lobel, *A Jewish-Sufi Dialogue: Philosophy and Mysticism in Baḥya Ibn Paquda's Duties of the Heart* (Philadelphia: University of Pennsylvania Press, 2007).
56 Baḥya ibn Paqūda, *The Book of Directions to the Duties of the Heart*, trans. Menahem Mansoor (London: Routledge and Kegan Paul, 1973), 89.

57 Georges Vajda, *La Théologie ascétique de Baḥya ibn Paqūda* (Paris: Imprimerie Nationale, 1947), 131–137.

58 Baḥya, *The Book of Directions to the Duties of the Heart*, 443–444.

59 For biographical details, see Samuel Rosenblatt, *The High Ways to Perfection of Abraham Maimonides* (New York: Columbia University Press, 1927), 40–58; Shlomo Dov Goitein, "Abraham Maimonides and His Pietist Circle," in *Jewish Medieval and Renaissance Studies*, ed. Alexander Altmann (Cambridge, MA: Harvard University Press, 1967), 145–164.

60 Rosenblatt, *The High Ways to Perfection of Abraham Maimonides*, 50.

61 Rosenblatt, *The High Ways to Perfection of Abraham Maimonides*, 51.

62 Rosenblatt, *The High Ways to Perfection of Abraham Maimonides*, 134–135.

63 Rosenblatt, *The High Ways to Perfection of Abraham Maimonides*, 138–139.

64 Fenton, *The Treatise of the Pool*, 115. I modify Fenton's translation somewhat here.

65 See Shlomo Dov Goitein, "A Jewish Addict to Sufism in the Time of Nagid David II Maimonides," *Jewish Quarterly Review* 44 (1953–54): 37–49; Paul Fenton, "The Literary Legacy of David ben Joshua, Last of the Maimonidean Nēgīdim." *Jewish Quarterly Review* 75, no. 1 (1984): 1–56.

66 Paul Fenton, "Judeo-Arabic Mystical Writings of the XIIIth-XIVth Centuries," in *Judeo-Arabic Studies: Proceedings of the Founding Conference of the Study of Judeo Arabic*, ed. Norman Golb (Amsterdam: Harwood, 1997), 87–102.

67 See, e.g., the sparse references to Sufism in his massive biography of Shabbetai Zvi: Gershom Scholem, *Sabbatai Sevi: The Mystical Messiah*, trans. R. J. Zwi Werblowsky (Princeton: Princeton University Press, 1973).

68 One exception is the work of Paul Fenton. See, e.g., his "Shabbatay Sebi and the Muslim Mystic Muhammad an-Niyazi," in *Approaches to Judaism in Medieval Times*, vol. 3, ed. David R. Blumenthal (Atlanta: Scholars Press, 1988), 81–88; idem, "A New Collection of Sabbatian Hymns," in *The Sabbatian Movement and Its Aftermath: Messianism, Sabbatianism and Frankism*, vol. 1, ed. Rachel Elior (Jerusalem: Magnes Press, 2001), 329–351 (in Hebrew); idem, "Influences soufies sur le développement de la Qabbale à Safed: l'exemple de la visitation des tombes," in *Etudes sur les terres saintes et les pèlerinages dans les religions monothéistes*, ed. D. Tollet (Paris: Honoré Champion Éditeur, 2012), 201–230.

69 Fenton, "Influences soufies sur le développement de la Qabbale à Safed," 203–204.

70 Fenton, "Influences soufies sur le développement de la Qabbale à Safed," 207–210. Paul Fenton, "Solitary Meditation in Jewish and Islamic Mysticism in the Light of a Recent Archeological Discovery," *Medieval Encounters* 2 (1995): 271–296.

71 Gershom Scholem, "Sprouting of the Horn of the Son of David: A New Source From the Beginnings of the Doenme Sect in Salonica," in *In the Time of Harvest: Essays in Honor of Abba Hillel Silver*, ed. Daniel Jeremy Silver (New York: Macmillan, 1963), 385.

72 Fenton, Shabbatay Sebi and the Muslim Mystic Muhammad an-Niyazi," 82–83.

73 See, e.g., Marc David Baer, *The Dönme: Jewish Converts, Muslim Revolutionaries, and Secular Turks* (Stanford: Stanford University Press, 2010), 5–12.

3 Resentment

The previous two chapters have revealed to just what an extent Judaism and Islam have been invested in one another, showing the manifold ways in which each has defined itself from, with, and against the other. One could quite easily make the case that the only reason these two religions appear the way they do today is on account of their deep historical involvement with one another. As certain developments took place in one religion – whether theological, mystical, philosophical, or even political – repercussions inevitably rippled out from the one and reached the shore of the other. Muslims and Jews formed business partnerships,[1] they read one another's work (albeit with more Jews reading Muslim texts than vice versa), and, for much of their history, they spoke a common language, of both the literal and metaphorical variety.

To show this, previous chapters have tried to avoid examining these exchanges wistfully or romantically, but instead as anxiety-producing, as moments wherein contacts with the other forced real and often uncomfortable self-examination and ultimately changes, be they real or imagined. Though the secondary literature often has no problem presenting these premodern Muslim-Jewish encounters using the larger frame of nostalgia, I have suggested that they instead produced apprehension, even unease, and that they reveal the all too real similarities between Jews and Muslims on the most basic of levels. When the earliest Muslims absorbed ideas that would later be labeled as "Jewish," for example, or when Jewish theologians articulated what they considered to be a normative rabbinic Judaism using the principles of Islamic *Kalam*, both used the other as an often fluid and unstable category to define the self.

Previous chapters have also emphasized that such interactions, and their results, did not emerge from some disembodied and reified Judaism bumping up against some equally disembodied and reified Islam. These encounters, in other words, did not take place outside of historical contexts, but firmly within them. It is precisely for this reason that these interactions, to reiterate, were anxiety-producing. There was no religion one could fall back on or turn to in solace. Their respective religions instead morphed and changed in the process. What the previous chapters have shown, I trust, is that the exchanges and interchanges between Jews and Muslims were embodied in real individuals and groups, in real historical moments, and part and parcel of the free exchange of ideas.

The present chapter, in contrast, seeks to show the fallout of these exchanges in the present. As mentioned in the Introduction, my goal is not to argue that the current violence between Palestinians and Israelis originated in the seventh or even the tenth century. Everyone who works on the conflict dates it to the rise of Zionism and the migration of Jews from Eastern Europe to Palestine in the 1880s. This I certainly do not doubt or wish to undermine. Despite this, however, I do want to connect the current anxiety that each has for the other to earlier anxieties, and to show how the struggle for self-definition – and the simultaneous abnegation of the other – is as alive today as it has ever been between these two groups. While I certainly realize that not all Muslims are Palestinian and indeed that not all Palestinians are even Muslim, I do wish to emphasize that the point at which Israelis and Palestinians confront one another today – and the ideology used to justify or legitimate the deprivation of human rights or even dehumanization – represents a set of encounters that is not unlike such contacts in the past.

This is certainly not to imply that proximity, interchange, and the confrontations that they inevitably produce must necessarily lead to the types of problems that currently beset these two communities. Far from it. It is, however, an attempt to think through a modern problem using a much larger historical frame than is customarily used. Such a frame, based as it is on the need for self-definition in the face of social and political messiness, is often missing in accounts of the Israeli-Palestinian conflict precisely because this longue durée is avoided. Instead, in our current political world "Jew" and "Muslim" are simply regarded as being as compatible as oil and water or as unproductive as the struggle between the need for nationalism and a desire for universal human rights. The current impasse in the Middle East between "Jew" and "Muslim," now reconfigured as "Israeli" and "Palestinian," seems to many to be a deep-seated religious conflict between two bitter enemies. It is instead, I want to suggest, but the latest attempt on behalf of Jews and Muslims to invoke their religious traditions to make sense of an encounter fraught with the nearness and concomitant apprehension of the other.

While I certainly do not want to deny that religion is complicit in the current conflict, it is important to remember that religion is an effective marker of difference. Religion is what sublimates social, and thus human, constructions to the level of metaphysics. What follows in this chapter is an attempt to show how the self-definitions examined in previous chapters continue to manifest themselves into the present and that, once again, religion is invoked as a way to ameliorate such tensions. On the one hand, this task is made easier since religion forms only one part of a much larger conflict; yet, on the other, it is made more difficult because it is often impossible to show where the "religious" ends and the "political" or the "ideological" begins. Yet this, it seems to me, is precisely the point: religion is once again invoked as the mechanism or as the catalyst whereby each group thinks about itself ultimately by thinking about the other.

In his 1984 *Jews of Islam*, the late historian Bernard Lewis could boldly title his final chapter "The End of the Tradition," by which he presumably refers to the end of the "tradition" of Jews and Muslims living peacefully together. Note also that he uses the definite article and the singular – *the tradition* – to refer to contact between Jews and Muslims as if they were a monolith, something that the foregoing analysis has avoided. Because he invokes the trope of symbiosis, when relations sour he sees this relationship as no longer working. Since I have avoided that metaphor and the language that structures it, I do not see this. Even when the two groups are in a state of conflict, they still interact with one another. Jews and Muslims, as the present chapter shows, continue to live together. Moreover, we cannot simply imagine their history as a lengthy set of peaceful interactions that simply sour when one side no longer desires cohabitation. Nevertheless, Lewis concludes his chapter, and the work as a whole, on a note of pessimism with the rise of Arab–Jewish revolts in Mandate Palestine. According to him:

> There have been many chapters in the long history of the Jewish people. Greek Alexandria was the home of Philo, Babylon of the Talmud, medieval Spain of a rich Hebrew literature; the Jews of Germany and Poland wrote major chapters in modern Jewish history. They have all gone, and only their monuments and memories

remain. The Judaeo-Islamic symbiosis was another great period of Jewish life and creativity, a long, rich, and vital chapter in Jewish history. It has now come to an end.[2]

Lewis, who is generally regarded as a neo-conservative thinker, bases his assessment on the rise of anti-Semitism in Arab lands and the gradual diminution of tolerance on the part of Arab leaders toward their Jewish minorities. In so doing, however, he largely overlooks Zionist transgression and its inability or unwillingness to deal with its minorities (Arab Israelis) or those it disenfranchises (Palestinians).[3] Pain for him, as it is for so many fixated on the modern iteration of this relationship, is imagined as unidirectional and even inevitable. Lewis's assessment, however, puts us right in the middle of the messy present, where each side finger-points directly at the other and cloaks itself in the mantle of its own perceived righteous victimhood.[4] Beyond the finger-pointing, the name-calling, and the violence, however, resides a deep-seated connection that the past can neither conceal nor make better. The webs that define the relationship between Jew and Muslim are, after all, subterranean and rarely perceptible in the light of day. This is the reason why they can be either romanticized or ignored altogether.

I thus disagree with the aforementioned comments of Lewis and would instead argue that this relationship does not come to an end precisely because it cannot. This relationship continues into the uncertain present as Jews and Muslims still invest the other with anxiety-inducing attributes that continue to drive the engines of self-definition. While such rhetoric may hold out the ephemeral hope of affirmation and denial, it ultimately proves fictive. Simplistic appeals to previous "golden ages" in an attempt to expiate current hatreds, thus, ignore the sheer messiness and utter complexity of real historical interactions between Jews and Muslims.

I certainly would not be so naïve as to claim that the study of this past will solve any, let alone all, of the problems of the present. This has not been my goal, nor do I think that it should be that of the scholarly endeavor. I will go so far, however, as to declare that an ignorance of that past plays into the hands of ethno-nationalists, demagogues, and their vehicles of dissemination that frequently masquerade as national presses. The primary difference between today and the premodern period is two-fold: (1) the Muslims I deal with in this chapter now live under Jewish (i.e., Israeli) control as opposed to vice versa; and (2) that identity is defined increasingly by occupation and oppression. Identity on each side of the boundary – security fence, apartheid wall, or whatever we choose to call it – is now constructed along ethno-nationalist lines and reinforced using the language of hate.

The present chapter thus seeks to move beyond politicized headlines and atavistic slogans, and instead show how the messy present continues to be invested in the process of self-definition. For this reason, I have opted not to use the past as some sort of romantic holdout for the present, but instead to show how the present, with obvious and various permutations, is but an extension of that past. In order to do this, however, it is necessary to examine the political complexity of the modern Middle East. I do this not to offer a primer of the Israeli-Palestinian conflict, but as a way to understand the cartography of a much larger modus vivendi.[5]

Zionism

Zionism must be situated against a larger romantic notion of people-hood common throughout Europe in the nineteenth century. Such a notion imagines a "people" as timeless and as having an eternal connection with a specific language, a unique history, and a particular piece of land. Though the land of Israel (*eretz Yisrael*) had always played a role in Jewish literature and liturgy, by the middle of the nineteenth century a national movement of the Jewish people arose, influenced as it was by other nationalisms, that supported the re-establishment of a Jewish national homeland. Two of the earliest ideologues of the fledgling movement were Rav Yehudah Alkalai (1798–1878) and Rav Zvi Hirsch Kallischer (1795–1874), both of whom sought to provide the religious justification for young Russian Jews to pick up and return to their ancestral homeland. For Alkalai, "We, as a people, are properly called Israel only in the land of Israel."[6] To achieve this, he recommended that "the soil of the Holy Land must be purchased from its non-Jewish owners."[7] According to Kallischer, "the redemption will begin by awakening support among the philanthropists and by gaining the consent of the nations to the gathering of some of the scattered of Israel into the Holy Land."[8] He also connects the need for a Jewish national home to the rising tide of nationalisms then sweeping throughout Europe:

> Why do the people of Italy and of other countries sacrifice their lives for the land of their fathers, while we, like men bereft of strength and

courage, do nothing? Are we inferior to all other peoples, who have no regard for life and fortune as compared with love of their land and nation? Let us take to heart the examples of the Italians, Poles, and Hungarians, who have laid down their lives and possessions in the struggle for national independence . . . All the other peoples have striven only for the sake of their own national honor; how much more should we exert ourselves, for our duty is to labor not only for the glory of our ancestors but for the glory of God who chose Zion![9]

Such comments would set the stage for and simultaneously be the fore-runner to Zionism, a movement that would increasingly pick up steam in the second half of the nineteenth century. Though many of those who would take up Alkalai's and Kallischer's charge were young and largely secular Jews from Russia and Eastern Europe, we see in their language some of the religious motivations behind the new movement. Jews were a people who had a deep-seated connection to a particular land that the Bible told them had been promised to them. As with other peoples who shared a common history and language, it was believed that they deserved their own national homeland. This call was all the more necessary, they believed, on account of the anti-Semitism in places wherein Jews found themselves. The Jews were a people without a land, so the early Zionist slogan went, and Palestine (they naively believed) was a land without a people. The religious views of Alkalai and Kallischer would certainly not be the norm among Zionists, however, on account of the traditional religious belief that it was the Messiah, and not Jewish political leaders, who would be responsible for the "ingathering of the exiles" to the Holy Land. Despite such early calls of religious promise and motivation, then, the earliest Zionists were primarily secular and, by definition, irreligious. Though all subsequent Zionists would stress this connection between land and peoplehood, religion – namely, Judaism – would tend to play a significant role only among religious Zionists, which I shall discuss shortly.

Those young Eastern European Jews who first made their way over to Palestine, which was at the time under the control of the Ottoman Empire, were known as *Hovevei Zion* ("lovers of Zion"). They were largely apolitical; their goal was to promote Jewish immigration and advance Jewish settlement in the area with the ultimate intent of establishing a Jewish national homeland there. What they all shared was the growing conviction that the Jews needed a land of their own to eradicate anti-Semitism and perceived Jewish passivity in the face of it. One of the movement's earliest ideologues was Leon Pinsker (1821–1869), who, among other things, wrote an influential work that was tellingly titled "Auto-Emancipation." According to him, the Jewish people

> lacks most of those attributes which are the hallmark of a nation. It lacks the characteristic national life which is inconceivable without a common language, common customs, and a common land. The Jewish people has no fatherland of its own, though many mother-lands; it has no rallying point, no center of gravity, no government of its own, no accredited representatives. It is everywhere a guest, and nowhere *at home*.[10]

To remedy this, Pinkser called for "the creation of a Jewish nationality, of a people living upon its own soil, the auto-emancipation of the Jews; their emancipation as a nation among nations by the acquisition of a home of their own."[11]

Despite the early Zionist slogans stating that the land of Palestine was unoccupied, there was a local population there. Though they were mainly rural, despite having important families in places like Jerusalem, early Zionists either ignored them or thought that their European ways would benefit them. Their new settlement (*Yishuv*) subsequently developed in a manner that was closed off from local Arab farmers and workers.[12] Rather than integration, there was a growing isolation between the two peoples. It was an isolation, moreover, that was unsustainable as the two populations grew and increasingly bumped up against one another, but often in ways that led to violence.

After this initial estrangement between Zionists and Arabs, only later to be renamed and reconfigured as Israelis and Palestinians, tensions mounted and manifested themselves most violently in the riots of 1920, 1921, and 1929. Such tensions reveal the growing frustration that each side had toward the other, with each imagining the other as an impedi-ment to their burgeoning national aspirations. Two social groups, largely unaware of their history of living together, now regarded the other as a problem to be ignored (as was the case of the treatment of Arabs among early Zionists) or resisted (vice versa). Zionists regarded the land as their ancestral homeland, whereas Arabs argued that it was theirs and that Jews were nothing more than European colonialists.

The result was, as the title of this chapter suggests, resentment. Each side imagined the other as a problem to be overcome and increasingly as an enemy to be defeated. This is the new phase, one that began in the early part of the twentieth century and continues into the present. Though religion was not responsible for the conflict, its ability to sublimate discourses of exclusion and hate to the level of divine speech would be increasingly folded into the impending conflict. It is this sublimation that provides for each group a sense of its own destiny and superiority, and confidence in the morality of its actions.

The necessity for differentiation witnessed in previous centuries thus finds a logical, if not necessarily natural, conclusion in the present. The growth, development, and mutual self-articulation encountered in previous chapters have, perhaps inevitably, perhaps not, led directly into the present, when relations between Muslim and Jew – now imagined to have morphed into a more secular conflict between peoples or ethnicities – have transformed into resentment and mutual dread. Once again we confront a moment of anxiety between these two groups. As with previous such moments we should not be surprised to find the need to legitimize the self and denigrate, if not actually dehumanize, the other.

Secular responses

As Theodor Herzl (1860–1904) and other early political Zionists increasingly began to assert the importance of a national homeland for the Jews of Europe by means of the political process, other Zionist thinkers emphasized the importance of creating a new cultural identity to unite Jews from disparate countries. Asher Ginsberg (aka Ahad ha-Am, 1856–1927), for example, stressed the necessity of a "Jewish state" and not simply a "state for the Jews" as imagined by the likes of Herzl. According to Ahad ha-Am, it was important to be vigilant against those forms of Zionism that have "no ideal beyond that of making the State supreme at home, respected abroad, and secure against aggression."[13] Such a vision, for him, "attached no importance to the spiritual aspect of national life, and [those who promulgated it] were almost prepared to desert the nation's spiritual ideal – 'to serve other gods' – if they thought there was any political advantage in doing so."[14]

To rectify this situation, Ahad ha-Am proposed that the Jews needed not just a political home, but a cultural one that would sustain and nurture the Jewish people. According to him:

> There can be no answer to our question until a new and compelling urge toward normalization springs up among us from within, from

our own Jewish life, and is communicated to the younger generation through education and literature . . . We must revitalize the idea of the national renascence, and use every possible means to strengthen its hold and deepen its roots, until it becomes an organic element in the Jewish consciousness and an independent dynamic force.[15]

Ahad ha-Am was also among the first Zionist thinkers to be attentive to the growing divide between Jews and Arabs. In an essay from 1891 titled "A Truth from Eretz Israel," for example, he wrote of problems that would result from Jewish settlers treating the Arabs with contempt, and warned the Zionists

not to provoke the anger of the native people by doing them wrong, how we should be cautious in our dealings with a foreign people among whom we returned to live, to handle these people with love and respect and, needless to say, with justice and good judgment. And what do our brothers do? Exactly the opposite! They were slaves in their diasporas, and suddenly they find themselves with unlimited freedom, wild freedom that only a country like Turkey can offer. This sudden change has planted despotic tendencies in their hearts, as always happens to former slaves ['*eved ki yimlokh* – when a slave becomes king – Proverbs 30:22]. They deal with the Arabs with hostility and cruelty, trespass unjustly, beat them shamefully for no sufficient reason, and even boast about their actions. There is no one to stop the flood and put an end to this despicable and danger-ous tendency. Our brothers indeed were right when they said that the Arab only respects he who exhibits bravery and courage. But when these people feel that the law is on their rival's side and, even more so, if they are right to think their rival's actions are unjust and oppressive, then, even if they are silent and endlessly reserved, they keep their anger in their hearts. And these people will be revengeful like no other.[16]

Despite warnings such as this, the *Yishuv* continued to develop at its own pace, with its own concerns, and largely divorced from those of its Arab neighbors. The two peoples now existed on their own separate trajectories. Rather than grow with one another as they had for centu-ries, they now turned on one another as self-definition in the face of the other now took a more urgent and sinister turn. With both sides largely divorced from one other, the repercussions of this solitude would only reverberate through the coming decades. The Arabs in response to their exclusion from the nascent Zionist settlement, and its growing economy, increasingly envisioned Zionists as a threat to their own national aspirations in the aftermath of the fall of the Ottoman Empire and at the time of the British Mandate (1923–1948).[17]

The Arab response

If those like Ahad ha-Am were conscious of the growing resentment of the local Arab inhabitants, certain Arab thinkers were increasingly cognizant of what they perceived to be European perfidy. George Antoninus (1891–1942), a Lebanese Christian and Cambridge-educated diplomat, is often regarded as one of the first articulators of Arab nationalism. In an important book titled *The Arab Awakening* (1938), Antoninus warns that "the establishment of a Jewish state in Palestine, or of a national home based on territorial sovereignty, cannot be accomplished without forcibly displacing the Arabs."[18] In so doing, he is particularly critical of Britain, whose "charity work" on behalf of Jews, he believes, will create real problems for the Arab majority in the region. He continues:

> The treatment meted out to Jews in Germany and other European countries is a disgrace to its authors and to modern civilisation; but posterity will not exonerate any country that fails to bear its proper share of the sacrifices needed to alleviate Jewish suffering and distress. To place the brunt of the burden upon Arab Palestine is a miserable evasion of the duty that lies upon the whole of the civilised world. It is also morally outrageous. No code of morals can justify the persecution of one people in an attempt to relieve the persecution of another. The cure for the eviction of Jews from Germany is not to be sought in the eviction of the Arabs from their homeland; and the relief of Jewish distress may not be accomplished at the cost of inflicting a corresponding distress upon an innocent and peaceful population.[19]

In the attempt to appease both sides, to fast forward our narrative, Britain suggested a partition of Palestine into two homelands – one Jewish, and one Arab – that would accompany its withdrawal in 1948. The British tried to do, then, what history had previously prevented: to separate with an artificially created line on a map two groups that had always lived within each other's midst. The results, as we shall see presently, were neither easy nor peaceful.

The Zionist continuum

Zionism is certainly not a monolith. What united its various forms, however, was a pressing need to solve what had become known as the "Jewish question," namely, what was the legal and social role of Jews (as a minority) within the modern European nation state. Most Zionists, from many different ideological stripes, desired a physical separation from Europe and the creation of their own nation state. The overwhelming goal was to normalize Jews, to make them into a nation or a people like any other nation or people. There were, as witnessed earlier, political Zionists, like Herzl, who sought a solution to the Jewish question in the *political* process of establishing a Jewish state. Then there were cultural Zionists, like Ahad ha-Am, who sought to solve the same problem but instead by the creation of a Jewish *culture* that would unify, nourish, and sustain Jews coming to the *Yishuv* from all over Europe. Yet others, such as labor Zionists, sought to solve the Jewish question with a Marxist ideal and the creation of a Jewish *worker* or peasant. Though even ideologues associated with this movement, it is perhaps worth noting, tended to be interested solely in the Jewish worker, and not the Arab one.

One of the more peaceful Zionist movements and one that seemed to be acutely aware of the impending conflict with Arabs was a group known as Brith Shalom ("The Covenant of Peace"). This organization, largely the work of a small group of German and American intellectuals, was created in 1925 with the aim of establishing peaceful coexistence between Arabs and Jews. It sought to do this by renouncing the Zionist aim of creating a Jewish state. In its stead it sought the establishment of a bi-national state, one wherein Jews and Arabs would have equal rights. It writes, for example, in its statutes (in English, Arabic, and Hebrew) that

> The object of the Association is to arrive at an understanding between Jews and Arabs as to the form of their mutual social relations in Palestine on the basis of absolute political equality of two anonymous peoples, and to determine the lines of their co-operation for the development of the country.[20]

Part of the organization's goal was to spread "verbal and written information among Jews and Arabs on the history and culture of both peoples, and the encouragement of friendly relations between them."[21]

For every action, though, there is a reaction. If the Zionism of Brith Shalom sought to create a bi-national state for Jews and Arabs, a more radical form was being constructed by the likes of Ze'ev Jabotinsky (1880–1940). In the same year as Brith Shalom was created, Jabotinsky broke away from the mainstream Zionist movement and established a new party called the Alliance of Revisionist-Zionists, a right-wing organization, that sought to champion a Jewish homeland on both sides of the River Jordan and to defend Zionist-Jewish interests, violently if necessary. According to Jabotinsky:

> We maintain unanimously that the economic position of the Palestinian Arab, under the Jewish colonization and owing to the Jewish colonization, has become the object of envy in all the surrounding Arab countries, so that the Arabs from those countries show a clear tendency to immigrate into Palestine. I have already shown to you that, in our submission, there is no question of ousting the Arabs. On the contrary, the idea is that Palestine on both sides of the Jordan should hold the Arabs, their progeny, *and* many millions of Jews. What I do not deny is that in the process the Arabs of Palestine will necessarily become a minority in the country of Palestine. What I do deny is that *that* is a hardship. It is not a hardship on any race, any nation, possessing so many National States now and so many National States in the future. One fraction, one branch of that race, and not a big one, will have to live in someone else's State.[22]

Here we see the beginnings of a call, one increasingly popular among right-wing Israeli politicians and their American supporters, that Israel has to be a Jewish state and that some proportion of the local Palestinian population can be or ought to be transferred to other Arab states in the region.

Religious Zionism

If the forms of Zionism just encountered sought to normalize Jews, to allow them to enter the historical process enjoyed by other nations, another form of Zionism was also taking shape, one that sought to emphasize the particularity and chosenness of the Jewish people and the holiness of the land that they believed had been divinely given to them by God. This form of Zionism would become increasingly popular after the 1967 war, the point at which Israel took Jerusalem (including the Old City) from Jordan. It is, moreover, the ideology behind the settler movement in the West Bank (occupied territories, if one is an Arab; Judea and Samaria, if one is a settler), which sees it as a religious obligation to settle the "holy" land. Despite its growing popularity since the late 1960s, the movement had its origins in the first part of the twentieth century. Abraham Isaac Kook (1865–1935), often known as Rav Kook, and the chief Ashkenazic Rabbi of Palestine, was heavily influenced by kabbalistic thought that, among other things, emphasized the individual Jew's active involvement in the redemptive process. It was Rav Kook who took these mystical properties and applied them to the land of Israel. At the same time, he also emphasized the spiritual superiority of the Jewish people. The conception of superiority, land, and religion – as the twentieth century has shown with some degree of regularity – is never a healthy triangulation.

Rav Kook argued that secular Zionists were, though unbeknownst to them, actually doing religious work because they were the ones laying the foundation for Israel's ultimate redemption.[23] Many of Rav Kook's teachings would be radicalized and popularized by his son, Rabbi Zvi Yehuda Kook (1891–1982), especially in the years after the Six Day War in 1967. The younger Kook, as we shall witness shortly, was among those who actively encouraged his religious followers to establish settlements throughout the West Bank and the Gaza Strip, many of which were granted official recognition by subsequent Israeli governments, both right and left.[24]

Two peoples at war, 1948–1967

Arab leadership refused to recognize the partition plan that occurred with British withdrawal from the Middle East in 1948, as set out in UN Resolution 181, arguing that they should not have to give up half of their land to what they perceived to be foreign transgressors. What had been a growing civil war between Zionists and Arabs prior to 1948 now became an interstate war, with the newly formed State of Israel at war with an army of Egyptian, Syrian, and Jordanian forces. This 1948 Arab-Israeli War resulted in Israeli victory, and Israel successfully took both the area that UN Resolution 181 had recommended for the proposed Jewish state as well as more than half of the area allocated for an Arab state. Transjordan took control of the remainder of the former British Mandate (what would become the West Bank after 1967), and Egypt took control of the Gaza Strip.

Despite this, no state was created for Palestinian Arabs. Numbers are hotly debated, but somewhere in the vicinity of 500,000 to 700,000 Palestinian Arabs fled or were expelled from their homes by the Israeli army, thereby creating what would become known as the Palestinian refugee problem. What became *yom ha-atzmaut* ("Independence Day") for Israelis now became known as *yawm al-nakhba* ("Day of Catastrophe") for Palestinians. Relations between Israel and its Arab neighbors never fully normalized, and, in 1967, they went to war with one another again. The result of this war – called the Six Day War or the June War, depending upon one's perspective – was a decisive Israeli victory, which, among other things, gave Israel control of the West Bank (including East Jerusalem), Gaza Strip, and the Golan Heights. This meant that the Palestinian Arabs of all of these areas now came under Israeli control.

These Arabs, soon to undergo a rebirth as Palestinians, essentially became stateless and lived under military occupation. Other Arab states in the area wanted little to do with them other than to show the inhumanness of the Israelis, and the Israelis did not know what to do with them for fear that, if they became Israeli citizens, Israel would quickly cease to have a Jewish majority. So the Palestinians, and just as importantly their voice, were in the years from 1948 to 1967 largely silenced or muted by other Arab countries in the region.

Jew and Muslim now became reminders to the other of the fear, the angst, and the potential for aggression after centuries of coexistence. What began, as witnessed in Chapter One, as the anxiety of sameness here emerges as the anxiety of difference. Again, though, the same process is at work: Israelis define themselves over and against those they perceive to be their opposite, just as Palestinians do the same. Each functions as the catalyst of self-definition for the other. While detractors not infrequently accuse the Palestinians of being an "invented" people, they are, of course, no more invented than Israelis or any other people.

Palestinian awakening

In the mid-1960s, a new generation of Palestinian nationalist movements began to organize. Especially important in this rise to national consciousness was the Palestine Liberation Organization (PLO), which formed in Cairo in 1964, soon thereafter coming under the leadership of Yasser Arafat.[25] When Egypt and Syria were unable to defeat Israel in the 1973 War, the PLO issued the following year its own ten point program with the aim of reasserting a Palestinian voice, liberating Palestine, and wrestling control of that objective from other Arab states, which they believed had coopted that goal for their own agendas. Point Two of its program, for example, reads:

> The Palestine Liberation Organization will employ all means, and first and foremost armed struggle, to liberate Palestinian territory and to establish the independent combatant national authority for the people over every part of Palestinian territory that is liberated. This will require further changes being effected in the balance of power in favor of our people and their struggle.[26]

In order to gain support, the leadership of the PLO sought to join their struggle to those of other "third-world" liberation struggles. Point Nine, for example, reads, "The Liberation Organization will strive to strengthen its solidarity with the socialist countries, and with the forces of liberation and progress throughout the world, with the aim of frustrating all the schemes of Zionism, reaction and imperialism."[27] Though the program met with opposition from other hardline Palestinian factions such as the Popular Front for the Liberation of Palestine (PFLP), which fought to eliminate Israel and feared that the program might lead to a peace treaty instead, the PLO continued to be the major voice of the Palestinian cause. Though the PLO emphasized armed struggle, it is perhaps worth noting in the present context that it did not exclude other means to achieve its ends.

Needless to say Israel perceived the ten point program as dangerous, fearing that the PLO would not honor any future compromise agreement between Israel and the Palestinian leadership. It raised the fear among Israelis, common into the present, that the Palestinian leadership spoke out of both sides of its mouth (or said one thing in Arabic to their supporters and something less bellicose in English to an international audience) and that it would simply exploit future Israeli territorial compromises in order to improve its position to attack Israel.

Later the same year the United Nations invited Yasser Arafat to address its General Assembly. Again, Arafat tied the fate of his people to other armed struggles of the oppressed against colonial overlords:

Great numbers of peoples, including those of Zimbabwe, Namibia, South Africa and Palestine, among many others, are still victims of oppression and violence. Their areas of the world are gripped by armed struggles provoked by imperialism and racial discrimination, both merely forms of aggression and terror. Those are instances of oppressed peoples compelled by intolerable circumstances into confrontation with such oppression. But wherever that confrontation occurs it is legitimate and just.[28]

After equating Zionism with racism and colonialism, he then moved to speak about the historical relations between Jews and Muslims. If not for the designs of Zionism, Arafat told the Assembly, and "if the immigration of Jews to Palestine had had as its objective the goal of enabling them to live side by side with us, enjoying the same rights and assuming the same duties, we would have opened our doors to them, as far as our homeland's capacity for absorption permitted."[29] He then went on to differentiate between Zionism and Judaism:

We do distinguish between Judaism and Zionism. While we maintain our opposition to the colonialist Zionist movement, we respect the Jewish faith. Today, almost one century after the rise of the Zionist movement, we wish to warn of its increasing danger to the Jews of the world, to our Arab people and to world peace and security. For Zionism encourages the Jew to emigrate out of his homeland and grants him an artificially-created nationality. The Zionists proceed with their terrorist activities even though these have proved ineffective. The phenomenon of constant emigration from Israel, which is bound to grow as the bastions of colonialism and racism in the world fall, is an example of the inevitability of the failure of such activities.[30]

Here, Arafat appeals indirectly to the past, to the shared destiny of Jews and Muslims in places like the Arabian Peninsula and Muslim Spain. We will witness such appeals again shortly in some of the writings produced by Hamas in the late 1980s, yet it is perhaps worth noting that it is, to be sure, a faulty invocation, one that is predicated on an imagined past in order to make little more than a politically expedient point in the present. The implication, of course, is that Jews – not Zionists – would be treated well in a Palestinian state so long as the former gave up any claims to political autonomy. Jews in the present should be like Jews in the past: aware of their subservience to Muslim or Arab hegemony. Such a claim was also an implicit acknowledgement of Palestinian weakness in the face of the military superiority of Israel. In light of Arafat's speech at the United Nations, the PLO was recognized as the sole legitimate representative of the Palestinian people and was granted observer status as a national liberation movement by the UN.

If the PLO threatened Israel with armed struggle, the latter regarded the PLO as a guerrilla – or, in the parlance of today, as a terrorist – organization that was committed to Israel's destruction. Palestinians launched attacks on Israel from Jordan and Lebanon, and engaged in high-profile hijackings of airplanes in the 1970s and early 1980s before Israel tried to eradicate the threat by, among other things, the invasion of Lebanon – including its capital of Beirut – in 1982.

Despite Israeli and American claims that they would never deal with the PLO, by the late 1980s and early 1990s it was clear that the PLO was the only legitimate group representing Palestinian demands. The PLO became, for example, part of the Israeli-Palestinian peace process, which culminated with the Oslo Accords in 1993. Despite a few years of peace in the aftermath of these Accords, by 2000 relations between Israelis and Palestinians had severely deteriorated with the eruption of the Second Intifada.

Today the conflict continues and, for the most part, revolves around whether or not Palestinians should be able to form their own separate country with its own government in a part of the territory that currently belongs to Israel. The question thus becomes, not unlike past iterations, how can each group live with and beside the other in a manner that takes into account past coexistence and mutual self-respect in the present.

Though the two groups define themselves against the other, as indeed they have since the beginning, their antagonism, self-definition, and demonization of the other now revolve less around theological self-definition than they do around one common piece of land. The issue now is: Can Israel and Palestine acknowledge the other's claims to territory in a manner that does not always culminate in mutual violence and instability? While some maintain that religion will be able to solve these problems, others argue that religion actually exacerbates such problems on account of its ability to portray oneself as morally right while simultaneously depriving the other of its humanity. While others point to the need to establish a Jewish or Muslim (or Arab) democracy, others argue that a democracy that is qualified by a religious or ethnic adjective cannot really function as a true democracy. These, of course, are questions that need to be addressed appropriately in the very near future.

From secularism to Islamism

Israel and the PLO, now the official representative of the Palestinian people, and the Palestinian Authority (PA), the civil government in the West Bank, have shown an ability, no matter how tortured, to work together. They have largely done so in the name of secular coexistence. Indeed, the PLO for much of its history has been defined by Marxist principles of revolution, with Islam playing little or no role in its principles. In an attempt to defang the PLO, Israel in the 1980s encouraged religious groups to meet, hoping they might offer an alternative to the militarism of the PLO.[31] One of the direct results of this encouragement was the creation in 1987 of the *Harakat al-Muqawamah al-Islamiyyah*, the "the Movement of Islamic Resistance," also known by its acronym of Hamas. The organization was founded to liberate Palestine, including modern day Israel, from occupation and to establish an Islamic state in the area that is now Israel, the West Bank, and the Gaza Strip.

Hamas's 1988 charter is a document rife with anti-Semitic statements that are subsequently invoked by critics of either that organization or Palestinian society more generally to show what they believe to be its true aims. As is typical of fundamentalist movements, Hamas imagines another time and another place as its high point. This, for many Islamic fundamentalists, is the time of Muhammad and his companions:

> By adopting Islam as its way of life, the Movement goes back to the time of the birth of the Islamic message, of the righteous ancestor, for Allah is its target, the Prophet is its example and the Koran is its constitution. Its extent in place is anywhere that there are Moslems who embrace Islam as their way of life everywhere in the globe. This being so, it extends to the depth of the earth and reaches out to the heaven.[32]

Those who formulated the Hamas charter would certainly not be interested in the type of social fluidity witnessed in Chapter One. What was such fluidity for us is, for them, a historic and sacred narrative. They instead imagine the Quran as sent directly from heaven to Muhammad and as the divine legislation meant to guide the life of every Muslim. Jews in their narrative – and this we did see in Chapter One in the discussion surrounding the biography of Muhammad – would have been the ones who threatened the community on account of their perfidy and unwillingness to embrace the message of Islam. The past, and again this should not surprise us, is selectively remembered to make a political point in the present.

The Hamas charter continues by excoriating Zionism. Article 8, for example, connects the struggle to liberate Palestine to the religious obligation to engage in *jihad* ("holy war"): "Allah is its target, the Prophet is its model, the Koran its constitution: Jihad is its path and death for the sake of Allah is the loftiest of its wishes."[33] Unwilling to distinguish between Zionism and Judaism, like the PLO, the charter then goes on to accuse Jews of a host of crimes that should be familiar to anyone with even a passing knowledge of anti-Semitic tropes:

> With their money, [the Jews] took control of the world media, news agencies, the press, publishing houses, broadcasting stations, and others. With their money they stirred revolutions in various parts of the world with the purpose of achieving their interests and reaping the fruit therein. They were behind the French Revolution, the Communist revolution and most of the revolutions we heard and hear about, here and there. With their money they formed secret societies, such as Freemasons, Rotary Clubs, the Lions and others in different parts of the world for the purpose of sabotaging societies and achieving Zionist interests. With their money they were able to control imperialistic countries and instigate them to colonize many countries in order to enable them to exploit their resources and spread corruption there . . . They were behind World War II, through which they made huge financial gains by trading in armaments, and paved the way for the establishment of their state. It was they who instigated the replacement of the League of Nations with the United Nations and the Security Council to enable them to rule the world through them. There is no war going on anywhere, without having their finger in it.[34]

This vein continues into Article 28:

> The Zionist invasion is a vicious invasion. It does not refrain from resorting to all methods, using all evil and contemptible ways to

achieve its end. It relies greatly in its infiltration and espionage operations on the secret organizations it gave rise to, such as the Freemasons, The Rotary and Lions clubs, and other sabotage groups. All these organizations, whether secret or open, work in the interest of Zionism and according to its instructions. They aim at undermining societies, destroying values, corrupting consciences, deteriorating character and annihilating Islam. It is behind the drug trade and alcoholism in all its kinds so as to facilitate its control and expansion.[35]

In order to garner support for its cause, Hamas here appeals to any discourse – anti-Judaism, anti-Semitism, colonialism, and even Orientalism[36] – that would seem to concur with its first principles. While its language is certainly abhorrent, it is important to recognize how the rhetoric of this document seeks to undermine the perceived political and religious supremacy of Israel and replace it with Hamas own ideological framework. Implicit in this is that Palestinians, and the Arab peoples more generally, can flourish only under Islam. Judaism, on their reading, can function only when it has Islam to help nourish it. Also implicit in this document is the notion that Zionism has reversed the historical record when Jews and Judaism functioned as little more than a minority under Muslim hegemony. According to Article 31:

The Islamic Resistance Movement is a humanistic movement. It takes care of human rights and is guided by Islamic tolerance when dealing with the followers of other religions. It does not antagonize anyone of them except if it is antagonized by it or stands in its way to hamper its moves and waste its efforts. . . . Under the wing of Islam, it is possible for the followers of the three religions – Islam, Christianity and Judaism – to coexist in peace and quiet with each other. Peace and quiet would not be possible except under the wing of Islam. Past and present history are the best witness to that . . . Islam confers upon everyone his legitimate rights. Islam prevents the incursion on other people's rights. The Zionist Nazi activities against our people will not last for long.[37]

Zionism and the modern State of Israel have inverted this historical process, and stood the natural order of Islam on its head. Hamas in the previous passage instead vows to restore this order with its offer to do what the State of Israel cannot do: to provide human rights to all who find themselves under Hamas's control. While I will leave it to others to prognosticate if this actually would occur, I only want to point out here how far we have come from the previous two chapters. While many Muslim ideologues rue the present fracture when compared to the perceived high point of the medieval caliphate, Jewish ideologues, in the aftermath of the Holocaust, are all too aware of the tragic consequences when Jews lack political autonomy and sovereignty.

The result is that the two groups seethe in their resentment for one another. While the past is but a distance, it is nonetheless omnipresent. Hamas accuses Judaism of being evil Zionists, and Israel accuses Palestinians (and often, by extension, all Muslims) of being fanatical terrorists. While the consequences are much greater today than they were in the past, the anxiety produced is still the result of these two groups trying to live beside one another and trying to make sense of themselves by making sense of the other.

Messy present

Hamas and Israel's response to it, including the violent confrontations between Israelis and Palestinians, bring us into the modern present. Much of this aggression once again stems from the shared space that Jews and Muslims occupy. This is perhaps best symbolized by what is alternately called a separation wall (Heb. *homat ha-hafrada*), a security fence (Heb. *geder ha-bitahon*), or an apartheid wall (Ar. *jidar al-fasl al-unsuri*), which, regardless of what we choose to call it, tries to do what history could not: to physically separate Jew and Muslim, Israeli and Palestinian, from one another. Despite the erection of this barrier, Israel continues to encroach on a future Palestinian state by building settlements. Just as religion plays a large part in Hamas's understanding of (and solution to) the conflict between these two groups, the settler movement, which seeks to annex all of the occupied territories to Israel, also invokes religion.

Here we need to return to the religious Zionist teachings of Rav Kook and, in particular, those of his son, Zvi Yehuda Kook. For him, non-Jews – and such a locution is, of course, code for "Palestinians" – impede the return of the Messiah because they pollute the land. Since Arabs are a pollutant they must necessarily be excised from the land, whether by invitation or by force. Just as Hamas seeks to erase all signs of Israeli presence on the land, so, too, do the settlers want to do the same to a Palestinian presence on the same land.

The secular State of Israel, including its army, could now be valorized as holy because both the state and its institutional apparatuses could be seen to be carrying out the redemptive task spoken about in the ancient Jewish sources. If non-Jews, including innocents, were killed in these "holy wars," this was acceptable because messianic fulfillment was morally superior to the death of non-Jews. Kook and his followers could rely theologically on Jewish mystical texts that held that non-Jews were not even fully human because they ascended from the side of evil (*sitra ahra*). This has led to a dualistic worldview wherein, according to Robert Eisen, there is "a clear division between Israel as the manifestation of goodness in the world, and the rest of the nations as the embodiment of all that was evil."[38]

Perhaps the most extreme version of this may be found in a theological tractate published in 2009 by Yitzhack Shapira and Yosef Elitzur, two rabbis associated with a seminary entitled Yeshiva Od Yosef Chai located in the West Bank.[39] Their controversial – and certainly non-normative – *Torat haMelekh* (Torah of the King) seeks, among other things, to provide guidance on how Israeli soldiers should conduct themselves in times of war.[40] Basing their arguments on a highly particularist reading of the traditional canons of Jewish law and theology, they state that under certain circumstances "non-involved" gentiles, including innocent women and children, may be preemptively killed. The reason why such force is allowed is because these innocents may, at some indeterminate point in the future, take up arms against Jews. Because of this future threat, they reason, it is permissible to kill these innocents in the present. Although Arabs are nowhere mentioned by name in the book, it is not difficult to see that such a work both legitimates and justifies the murder of innocent Palestinians (including children) for the sake of some self-perceived religious struggle between Jew and non-Jew.[41]

Just to make sure that we do not emphasize the inclusive reading at the expense of the exclusive one, it is worth noting that the authors of *Torat haMelekh* believe that individuals who violate the Noahide commandments ought to be murdered. Within this context and to show that this is not just a theoretical debate that plays out in medieval sources, it is worth pointing out that many settlers in the ultra-right religious Zionist movement adamantly believe that the Palestinians have violated the Noahide prohibition against theft because they have stolen land from Jews.

The authors of *Torat haMelekh*, no less than those who penned the Hamas charter, certainly challenge our liberal reading both of religion and of human nature. They nevertheless reveal the stakes, what I have here called the resentment, between two groups (or peoples or religions, or whatever we choose to call them) as they struggle over one piece of land that each believes rightfully belongs to it.

Conclusions

Unlike previous chapters, the present one shows Jew and Muslim in their angriest and most resentful encounters. Though, as in the previous chapters, this anger and resentment further reveal to us both the complexity and sheer messiness of social action between groups that appeal to both Judaism and Islam. The modern period also shows us that these two religious traditions, but especially those who practice them, have always been intertwined with one another. To say that this encounter has stopped, as Lewis does, or to imply that some originary symbiosis has dried up, as Goitein does, does not aid us in our analysis.

The encounter continues, however, as it inevitably must. To mark its abrupt terminus is nothing less than the historian's conceit. Continue it must because Jew and Muslim, whether imagined as Israeli and Palestinian or some other configuration, still share an epistemic space and the same need to articulate theological clarity in the face of what is perceived to be impending chaos. In so doing, both persevere in using the same tropes as they did in the past. The past continues, depending on the narrative one chooses, to enchant or to haunt. These tropes, as I trust the present chapter has made increasingly clear, help to define the self in the imposing shadow that the other casts, and facilitate the desire to carve out a clearing – ontological in previous chapters, geographic in the present – for oneself at the expense of the other. All the while, however, the rhetoric, if somewhat more secular and militant than witnessed in the past, remains. Jew and Muslim continue to need one another for the purpose of their own fulfillment. Without the other to think with or to think about, each reverts to a moment of repose, a self-imposed exile.

The great paradox is that neither Muslim nor Jew in the present is particularly interested in this past. The focus instead is solely on the animosity in the present. While I doubt even a passing knowledge of the past on the part of today's antagonists would mean much, certainly not a solution to the problems that lay ahead, it certainly illumines some of the uncertain terrain.

Notes

1 Though I have not focused on the Cairo Genizah here, I would refer the interested reader to Ackerman-Lieberman, *The Business of Identity*. See also David M. Freidenreich, *Foreigners and Their Food: Constructing Otherness in Jewish, Christian, and Islamic Law* (Berkeley: University of California Press, 2011).

2 Lewis, *The Jews of Islam*, 190.

3 One does not have far to look for the latter either, however. See, in this regard, Mark Tessler, *A History of the Israeli-Palestinian Conflict*, 2nd ed. (Bloomington: Indiana University Press, 2009), 185–264.

4 See Benny Morris, *Righteous Victims: A History of the Zionist–Arab Conflict, 1881–2001* (New York: Vintage, 2001), 676–694.

5 I prefer to refer to this as the "Israeli-Palestinian conflict" because the alternative phrases – "Arab-Israeli conflict" or "Jewish-Muslim conflict" – have too many inverse repercussions. The former, for example, implies a David and Goliath story wherein tiny Israel is surrounded by hostile countries that want to attack it, something that is patently not true in the modern period given Israel's military superiority. The latter implies that the conflict is motivated by religion. While I am certainly more amenable to the religious aspects of the conflict in this chapter, I would certainly not claim that the conflict is solely about religion, but rather that religion plays a role – a small, but not insignificant role – in it. And it is incumbent upon us to appreciate that role.

6 Yehudah Alkalai, "The Third Redemption (1843)," in *The Zionist Idea: A Historical Analysis and Reader*, ed. Arthur Hertzberg (Philadelphia: Jewish Publication Society of America, 1997), 105–107, at 107.

7 Alkalai, "The Third Redemption," 105.

8 Zvi Hirsch Kallischer, "Seeking Zion (1862)," in *The Zionist Idea*, 111–114, at 111.

9 Kallischer, "Seeking Zion," 114.

10 Leon Pinkser, "Auto-Emancipation: An Appeal to His People by a Russian Jew," in *The Zionist Idea*, 181–198, at 183.

11 Pinkser, "Auto-Emancipation," 198.

12 Neil Caplan, *The Israel-Palestine Conflict: Contested Histories* (Malden and Oxford: Wiley-Blackwell, 2010), 66–67.

13 Ahad ha-Am, "Flesh and Spirit (1904)," in *The Zionist Idea*, 256–260, at 257.

14 Ahad ha-Am, "Flesh and Spirit," 257.

15 Ahad ha-Am, "The Law of the Heart (1894)," in *The Zionist Idea*, 251–255, at 255.

16 Ahad ha-Am, "A Truth from Eretz Israel," in *Wrestling With Zion: Progressive Jewish-American Responses to the Israeli-Palestinian Conflict*, eds. Tony Kushner and Alisa Solomon (New York: Grove Press, 2003), 14–16, at 15.

17 Mention could also be made here of the seeming British desire to try to appease both Zionists and Arabs. The Balfour Declaration (1917), some 67 words long, promised the establishment of a "national home for the Jewish

people." Whereas the correspondence between George McMahon, the British High Commissioner in Cairo, and Sharif Husayn of Mecca in 1915–1916 seemed to promise the same to the Arabs. This "twice promised land," as it is sometimes called, only exacerbates these problems. Each group, perhaps not surprisingly, chooses to emphasize only the documents and/or UN resolutions that support its claim while simultaneously either ignoring or writing off those that do not.

18 George Antoninus, *The Arab Awakening: The Story of the Arab National Movement* (London: Routledge, 2010 [1938]), 410.
19 Antoninus, *The Arab Awakening*, 411.
20 "Brith Shalom Statues," in *A Land of Two Peoples: Martin Buber on Jews and Arabs*, ed. Martin Buber (Chicago: University of Chicago Press, 2005 [1983]), 74.
21 "Brith Shalom Statutes," 74.
22 Vladimir Jabotinsky, "Evidence Submitted to the Palestine Royal Commission (1937)," *The Zionist Idea*, 559–570, at 562.
23 Aviezer Ravitzky, *Messianism, Zionism, and Jewish Religious Radicalism*, trans. Michael Swirsky and Jonathan Chipman (Chicago: University of Chicago Press, 1996), 101–125.
24 Ravitzky, *Zionism, and Jewish Religious Radicalism*, 80–84.
25 Tessler, *A History of the Israeli-Palestinian Conflict*, 427–437.
26 Qtd., with modification, in *The Israel-Arab Reader: A Documentary History of the Middle East*, 7th rev ed., eds. Walter Laqueur and Barry Rubin (London and New York: Penguin, 2008), 162.
27 Qtd., with modification, in *The Israel-Arab Reader*, 163.
28 Yasser Arafat, "Address to the UN General Assembly." The transcript may be found online at https://unispal.un.org/DPA/DPR/unispal.nsf/0/A238EC7A3E13EED18525624A007697EC.
29 Arafat, "Address to the UN General Assembly."
30 Arafat, "Address to the UN General Assembly."
31 Tessler, *A History of the Israeli-Palestinian Conflict*, 695.
32 Article 5, online at http://avalon.law.yale.edu/20th_century/hamas.asp.
33 Article 5, online at http://avalon.law.yale.edu/20th_century/hamas.asp.
34 Article 22, online at http://avalon.law.yale.edu/20th_century/hamas.asp.
35 Article 28, online at http://avalon.law.yale.edu/20th_century/hamas.asp.
36 Article 15, for example, reads:

> It is important that basic changes be made in the school curriculum, to cleanse it of the traces of ideological invasion that affected it as a result of the orientalists and missionaries who infiltrated the region following the defeat of the Crusaders at the hands of Salah el-Din (Saladin).

37 Article 31, online at http://avalon.law.yale.edu/20th_century/hamas.asp.
38 Robert Eisen, *The Peace and Violence of Judaism: From the Bible to Modern Zionism* (Oxford and New York: Oxford University Press, 2011), 150.
39 See my "Theology: The Articulation of Orthodoxy," 87–89.
40 Yitzack Shapira and Yosef Elitzur, *Torat haMelekh, Part One: Criminal Laws Between Israel and Others* [in Hebrew] (Yeshivat Od Yosef Chai, 2009).

41 Instead of mentioning Arabs, the authors use "children of Noah." In their synopsis of Chapter One, for example, they write:

> In this chapter we deal with the notion that the prohibition of "do not murder" [*lo tirtzach*] does not apply to non-Jews. And, the prohibition of Jews killing non-Jews is learned from the prohibition given to the offspring of Noah against killing others. In the appendixes of the chapter we deal with another principle that the Jews are obligated in the commandments given to Noah.
>
> (Shapira and Elitzur, *Torat haMelekh*, 17)

Conclusion
Disengagement

The previous three chapters have charted the complex relation between two religions genuinely thought to be incompatible with one another in the modern period. Note, however, that I have avoided invoking the theme, so popular among comparative religionists, of imagining discrete religions or religious mentalities colliding in some ahistorical vacuum. I have also tried to avoid the language of who had what first, who influenced whom, or who took what from whom. Instead I have chosen to focus on social and historical actors who made – and indeed continue to make – appeals to what they perceive to be the eternal truths provided by these two religions. But the religions themselves have very little to do with the story I have tried to tell here. They are, on my telling, little more than abstract doctrines that do not – indeed cannot – exist apart from the human agents who both articulate them and, once articulated, hold them.

It is quite common to hear something like the following: "Why can't Jews and Muslims get along on account of their similarities and their close historical relationship?" I have hopefully shown how such a statement is both problematic and patently false. There was no Eden in which these two groups miraculously got along unscathed by the general wear and tear of social interactions. There have always been skirmishes over self-definition and the concomitant anxiety that such endeavors produce. Despite this, politicians, journalists, and even scholars have evoked the past as an antidote to current ills, and indeed have repeated this evocation with some degree of regularity. It is, however, unhelpful. It implies not only that things were good or better in remote periods and geographies, but also that the past must necessarily give definition to the present. Rather than engage in such a fictive reading of the historical record, the present study has instead focused on just how complicated the relations between these two social groups have been and continue to be.

Slogans that invoke symbiosis or convivencia reveal more about uncertain presents than they do about the past. Unfortunately the present – with its desire to posit a stable Judaism and Islam from the earliest period of their cohabitation, its willingness to construct discrete essences even in the medieval period or even in the midst of the Israeli-Palestinian conflict – has obscured our vision. In response to this status quo, I have tried to revisit the familiar with a set of new questions, thereby hopefully making it much more complex and thus unfamiliar.

In Chapter One, to repeat, this meant thinking about nascent Islam *and* nascent Judaism – both representative of some generic Near Eastern monotheism – growing and developing in tandem with one another. It was not the case, so often repeated in our textbooks, that a stable Judaism helped to birth a fledgling Islam. If anything, I suggested, Judaism needed Islam as much as vice versa in order to begin to articulate its truth claims and thereby firm up what would become normative rabbinic Judaism.

Chapter Two then took these truth claims as its main point of departure. Such claims, contrary to popular belief, did not fall from heaven, and neither were they written in a book imagined as sacred or as already preexistent by the time Jews and Muslims first interacted on the Arabian Peninsula. Rather, I suggested that, once again, such truth claims came into existence only as Islamic and Jewish thinkers thought about themselves by means of thinking about the other. Within this larger context, "Jew" and "Judaism" became a set of tropes upon which Muslim theologians could think about themselves and their tradition by articulating that which they were not, and subsequently define those Muslim groups that could be labeled as "heterodox" (e.g., the Shia). In like manner, "Muslim" and "Islam," in the hands of Jewish thinkers, became a way to articulate what Judaism should be. In each case, the other became the catalyst for self-definition.

Chapter Three took some of these earlier attempts at self-definition and, in particular, the manifold ways that Jews and Muslims thought about the other (to think about themselves) and showed how, despite the temporal and geographic distance, the same principles are still in effect. Notwithstanding such distance and the secular overlay of the modern conflict, the basic sociological and psychological need to think about the self by thinking about the other remains intact.

Jews and Muslims – or, alternatively, Israelis and Palestinians or even Israelis and Arabs – have been intertwined with one another, developing in tandem, for much of the past thirteen hundred years. Certainly 1948 marked a new turn in that relationship; nevertheless it is but one significant date among countless others. Obviously I do not think that an appreciation of this past will solve the conflict, let alone open up before us a vista of hope. My reason for documenting it here, and doing so moreover in a manner that departs from more mainstream treatments, is to show that the relationship between these religions, or the peoples that hold them, is much more complex, subterranean, and even helix-like than we are accustomed to believe.

Jews and Muslims, then, have been in conversation with one another ever since Muhammad began his prophetic career at the beginning of the seventh century. While other religious traditions have certainly been in conversation with one another over the centuries – Buddhism and Hinduism, and Judaism and Christianity, come immediately to mind – I would argue that no two religions have thought with, from, and about the other to the same extent that Islam and Judaism have. In order to appreciate this, however, we have to avoid facile comparisons that work with static notions of what Judaism and Islam mean, whether at the beginning, during the period of medieval florescence, or now at the time of what certainly appears to be their nadir.

Though I have refused to look into a crystal ball here or to use the past as a way to mitigate today's hatred, I wish to conclude with the observation that perhaps what these two groups need now more than anything is solitude. There now sits between them an exhaustion caused by centuries of cohabitation. The past 150 years have witnessed destruction, violence, and death on both sides of what has always been an artificial border. It does not seem, moreover, that this violence will dissipate anytime in the near future.

Whenever I am asked how the current conflict can be solved, I always point to two solutions. Both are predicated on the notion that the situation today is untenable and that it is not okay to occupy another people's land. The first is what I like to call the creation of "Canada in the Middle East." This would mean making Israel/Palestine – perhaps it would have to be renamed – into a secular country wherein every citizen, regardless of religion or ethnicity, is granted the same rights and freedom as every other citizen. Religion would be something done inside houses of worship, but play no role in the public sphere or in government ministries.

Such a proposed solution, however, would make no room for religion, either Islam or Judaism, despite the fact that these have been the twin engines that have powered the interaction between these two peoples for centuries. It would reduce religion to the private sphere, not to mention the fact that it would undoubtedly antagonize many on both sides. However, it is certainly more attractive than the other "one-state" solution proposed by some on the Israeli side, which is tantamount to a full-scale annexation of Palestinian land.[1]

The other proposed solution is that of the "two-state" option. This usually means Israel giving up land it took during the 1967 war and returning it to Palestinians, who could then use it to create their own nation state. While this would still enable each to retain its own religious identity and presumably with a sizable religious minority composing the other, the mutual recrimination witnessed in the previous chapter now begins to bubble again to the surface. Israelis – invoking documents such as the Hamas charter – accuse Palestinian leadership of acting in bad faith, and Palestinians accuse Israelis of suffocating them with settlements.

Again, we return to our messy present. If neither side is prepared to budge – or, alternatively, if one side refuses to be a partner for peace – the conflict will simply reproduce itself every generation with increasingly murderous consequences. Just as each side used the other to define itself through their long history of cohabitation, now both are equally to blame for the mess in which they find themselves.

It may seem odd to end a volume devoted to the historical and sociological interconnections between Jews and Muslims with a call for solitude or even disengagement. What seems clear, however, is that for each group not only to survive, but to flourish, there needs to be mutual respect, dignity, and, with obvious exceptions, equality. This is a modern story, however, and not something we can simply cherry-pick from the premodern period. The problem today is that neither side is willing – with obvious exceptions, such as individuals, NGOs, or organizations devoted to peace – to afford these traits to the other. The discrepancy in power is simply too great at the current moment.

Perhaps it was the vision of Brith Shalom that represents the missed opportunity in this study. Its goal, it will be recalled from the previous chapter, was to encourage "verbal and written information among Jews and Arabs on the history and culture of both peoples, and the encouragement of friendly relations between them."[2] It is this information, unfortunately, that is lacking on both sides. It is information, moreover, that the present study has tried to highlight.

Jews and Muslims, Judaism and Islam, have always gotten along best when the framers of each tradition sought to firm up the epistemological border between them. Unfortunately today the main border between them is usually an 8-meter iron wall, with a 60-meter exclusion area that snakes around 1967 borders without fully respecting them.

Perhaps time apart will lead to a newfound respect.

Notes

1 Though, of course, it is not referred to in such circles as "Palestinian land," but instead as "Judea and Samaria," the biblical names for it. Implicit in this is that the land is not Palestinian at all, but Jewish.
2 "Brith Shalom Statutes," 74.

Bibliography

Ackerman-Lieberman, Phillip I. *The Business of Identity: Jews, Muslims, and Economic Life in Medieval Egypt*. Palo Alto: Stanford University Press, 2013.

Adang, Camilla. *Muslim Writers on Judaism and the Hebrew Bible: From Ibn Rabban to Ibn Hazm*. Leiden: Brill, 1996.

Ahroni, Reuben. *Yemenite Jewry: Origins, Culture and Literature*. Bloomington: Indiana University Press, 1986.

Alfarabi. "The Enumeration of the Religious Sciences." In *Medieval Political Philosophy*, edited by Ralph Lerner and Muhsin Mahdi. Ithaca: Cornell University Press, 1963.

al-Ghabban, Ali Ibrahim et al. *Routes d'Arabie: Archéologie et Histoire du Royaume d'Arabie Saoudite*. Paris: Somogy, 2010.

al-Jabbār, Abd. *A Critique of Christian Origins*. Edited, translated, and annotated by Gabriel Said Reynolds and Samir Khalil Samir. Provo: Brigham Young University Press, 2010.

Antoninus, George. *The Arab Awakening: The Story of the Arab National Movement*. London: Routledge, 2010 [1938].

Ashtor, Eliyahu. *The Jews of Moslem Spain*, 3 vols. Translated by Aaron Klein and Jenny Machlowitz Klein. Philadelphia: Jewish Publication Society of America, 1973–1984.

Avicenna. *Kitāb al-Ishārāt wa'l-Tanbihāt*, 3 vols. Edited by S. Dunya. Cairo: Dār al-Maʿārif bi-Miṣr, 1960.

Baer, Marc David. *The Dönme: Jewish Converts, Muslim Revolutionaries, and Secular Turks*. Stanford: Stanford University Press, 2010.

Bayart, Jean-François. *The Illusion of Cultural Identity*. Translated by Steven Rendell et al. Chicago: University of Chicago Press, 2005.

Berg, Herbert. *The Development of Exegesis in Early Islam: The Authenticity of Muslim Literature From the Formative Period*. London: Curzon, 2000.

Bowersock, Glen W. *The Throne of Adulis: Red Sea Wars on the Eve of Islam*. Oxford and New York: Oxford University Press, 2013.

Boyarin, Daniel. *Border Lines: The Partition of Judaeo-Christianity*. Philadelphia: University of Pennsylvania Press, 2014.

Brann, Eva T. H. *The World of the Imagination: Sum and Substance*. Lanham: Rowman and Littlefield, 1991.

Brann, Ross. *Power in the Portrayal: Representations of Jews and Muslims in Eleventh- and Twelfth-Century Islamic Spain*. Princeton: Princeton University Press, 2002.

Buber, Martin. *A Land of Two Peoples: Martin Buber on Jews and Arabs*. Chicago: University of Chicago Press, 2005 [1983].

Caplan, Neil. *The Israel-Palestine Conflict: Contested Histories*. Malden and Oxford: Wiley-Blackwell, 2010.

Cook, Michael. *Commanding Right and Forbidding Wrong in Islamic Thought*. Cambridge: Cambridge University Press, 2010.

———. "The Origins of the *Kalām*." *Bulletin of the School of Oriental and African Studies* 43 (1980): 32–43.

Corbin, Henry. *Avicenna and the Visionary Recital*. Princeton: Princeton University Press, 1960.

———. *Creative Imagination in the Sufism of Ibn Arabi*. Translated by Ralph Manheim. Princeton: Princeton University Press, 1969.

Crone, Patricia, and Michael Cook. *Hagarism: The Making of the Islamic World*. Cambridge: Cambridge University Press, 1977.

Dagron, Gilbert, and Vincent Déroche. "Juifs et Chrétiens dans l'Orient du VIIe siècle." *Traveaux et mémoires* 11 (1991): 17–273.

Dakake, Maria Massi. *The Charismatic Community: Shi'ite Identity in Early Islam*. Albany: State University of New York Press, 2007.

Dohrmann, Natalie, and Annette Yoshiko Reed. "Introduction." In *Jews, Christians, and the Roman Empire: The Poetics of Power in Late Antiquity*, edited by N. Dohrmann and A. Y. Reed, 1–22. Philadelphia: University of Pennsylvania Press, 2013.

Donner, Fred M. *Narratives of Islamic Origins: The Beginning of Islamic Historical Writings*. Princeton: Darwin Press, 1998.

Eisen, Robert. *The Peace and Violence of Judaism: From the Bible to Modern Zionism*. Oxford and New York: Oxford University Press, 2011.

Fenton, Paul. "Influences soufies sur le développement de la Qabbale à Safed: l'exemple de la visitation des tombes." In *Etudes sur les terres saintes et les pèlerinages dans les religions monothéistes*, edited by D. Tollet, 201–230. Paris: Honoré Champion Éditeur, 2012.

———. "Judeo-Arabic Mystical Writings of the XIIIth-XIVth Centuries." In *Judeo-Arabic Studies: Proceedings of the Founding Conference of the Study of Judeo Arabic*, edited by Norman Golb, 87–102. Amsterdam: Harwood, 1997.

———. "The Literary Legacy of David ben Joshua, Last of the Maimonidean Nēgīdim." *Jewish Quarterly Review* 75, no. 1 (1984): 1–56.

———. "A New Collection of Sabbatian Hymns." In *The Sabbatian Movement and Its Aftermath: Messianism, Sabbatianism and Frankism*, vol. 1, edited by Rachel Elior, 329–351. Jerusalem: Magnes Press, 2001.

————. "Shabbatay Sebi and the Muslim Mystic Muhammad an-Niyazi." In *Approaches to Judaism in Medieval Times*, vol. 3, edited by David R. Blumenthal, 81–88. Atlanta: Scholars Press, 1988.

————. "Solitary Meditation in Jewish and Islamic Mysticism in the Light of a Recent Archeological Discovery." *Medieval Encounters* 2 (1995): 271–296.

Fernandez-Morera, Dario. *The Myth of Andalusian Paradise: Muslims, Christians, and Jews Under Islamic Rule in Muslim Spain*. Wilmington: ISI Books, 2016.

Fishman, Talya. *Becoming the People of the Talmud: Oral Torah as Written Tradition in Medieval Jewish Cultures*. Philadelphia: University of Pennsylvania Press, 2011.

Frank, Daniel. *Search Scripture Well: Karaite Exegesis and the Origins of the Jewish Bible Commentary in the Islamic East*. Leiden: Brill, 2004.

Freidenreich, David M. *Foreigners and Their Food: Constructing Otherness in Jewish, Christian, and Islamic Law*. Berkeley: University of California Press, 2011.

Friedlander, Israel. "Abdallah b. Saba, der Begründer der Shiʿa, und sein jüdischer Ursprung." *Zeitschrift für Assyriologie* 23 (1909): 296–327 and 24 (1910): 1–46.

Gajda, Iwona. *Le royaume de Ḥimyar à l'époque monothéiste*. Paris: Académie des Inscriptions et Belles-Lettres, 2009.

Gaon, Saadia. "The Book of Doctrines and Beliefs." In *Three Jewish Philosophers: Philo, Saadya Gaon, Yehuda Halevi*. Translated by Hans Lewy, Alexander Altmann, and Isaac Heinemann, 3rd ed. London: The Toby Press, 2006.

Geiger, Abraham. *Judaism and Islam*. Translated by F. M. Young. Madras: MDC-SPK Press, 1835; repr. New York: Ktav, 1970.

Goitein, Shlomo Dov. "Abraham Maimonides and His Pietist Circle." In *Jewish Medieval and Renaissance Studies*, edited by Alexander Altmann, 145–164. Cambridge, MA: Harvard University Press, 1967.

————. "A Jewish Addict to Sufism in the Time of Nagid David II Maimonides." *Jewish Quarterly Review* 44 (1953–54): 37–49.

————. *Jews and Arabs: Their Contacts Through the Ages*. New York: Schocken, 1955.

————. *A Mediterranean Society: The Jewish Communities of the Arab World as Portrayed in the Documents of the Cairo Geniza*, 6 vols. Berkeley: University of California Press, 1967–93.

————. "New Documents From the Cairo Geniza." In *Homenaje a Millas-Vallicrosa*, vol. 1, 717–720. Barcelona: Consejo Superior de Investigaciones Científicas, 1954.

————. *The Yemenites: History, Social Orders, Spiritual Life*. Edited by Menachem Ben-Sasson. Jerusalem: Yad Ben-Zvi and the Hebrew University of Jerusalem, 1983.

Goldziher, Ignaz. *Introduction to Islamic Theology and Law*. Translated by Andras and Ruth Hamori. Princeton: Princeton University Press, 1981.

Graetz, Heinrich. *History of the Jews*, vol. 3. Philadelphia: Jewish Publication Society of America, 1956 [1856].

Halevi, Judah. *Kitāb al-radd wa'l-dalīl fī'l-dīn al-dhalīl* (al-kitāb al-khazarī). Edited by David H. Baneth and Haggai Ben-Shammai. Jerusalem: Magnes Press, 1977. English translation: *The Kuzari: An Argument for the Faith of Israel*. Translated by Hartwig Hirschfeld. New York: Schocken, 1964. French translation: *Le Kuzari: Apologie de la religion méprisée*. Translated by Charles Touati. Paris: Verdier, 1994.

Hamidullah, Muhammad. *The First Written Constitution in the World: An Important Document of the Time of the Holy Prophet*, 3rd rev. ed. Lahore: Sh. Muhammad Ashraf, [1394] 1975.

Hatke, George. *Aksum and Nubia: Warfare, Commerce, and Political Fictions in Ancient Northeast Africa*. New York: New York University Press, 2013.

Healey, John. *The Nabataean Tomb Inscriptions of Mad'in Salih*. Oxford: JSS, 1993.

Hertzberg, Arthur, ed. *The Zionist Idea: A Historical Analysis and Reader*. Philadelphia: Jewish Publication Society of America, 1997.

Hoyland, Robert. *Seeing Islam as Others Saw It: A Survey and Evaluation of Christian, Jewish, and Zoroastrian Writings on Early Islam*. Princeton: Darwin Press, 1997.

Hughes, Aaron W. *Abrahamic Religions: On the Uses and Abuses of History*. Oxford and New York: Oxford University Press, 2012.

———. *The Art of Dialogue in Jewish Philosophy*. Bloomington: Indiana University Press, 2008.

———. "Religion Without Religion: Integrating Islamic Origins Into Religious Studies." *Journal of the American Academy of Religion* 85, no. 4 (2017): 867–888.

———. *Shared Identities: Medieval and Modern Imaginings of Judeo-Islam*. Oxford and New York: Oxford University Press, 2017.

———. *Texture of the Divine: Imagination in Medieval Islamic and Jewish Thought*. Bloomington: Indiana University Press, 2004.

———. "Theology: The Articulation of Orthodoxy." In *The Routledge Handbook of Muslim-Jewish Relations*, edited by Josef Meri, 77–94. London and New York: Routledge, 2016.

Hughes, Aaron W., and James T. Robinson, eds. *Medieval Jewish Philosophy and Its Literary Forms*. Bloomington: Indiana University Press, 2019.

Ibn Ezra, Abraham. *Religious Poems of Ibn Ezra*. Edited by Israel Levin. Jerusalem: Israel Academy of Sciences and Humanities, 1975.

Ibn Ishaq. *Life of Muhammad: A Translation of Ibn Ishaq's Sirat Rasul Allah*. Edited and translated by Alfred Guillaume. Oxford: Oxford University Press, 1955.

Ibn Kammuna. *Ibn Kammūna's Examination of the Three Faiths: A Thirteenth-Century Essay in the Comparative Study of Religion*. Translated by Moshe Perlmann. Berkeley: University of California Press, 1971.

Ibn Paquda, Baḥya. *The Book of Directions to the Duties of the Heart*. Translated by Menahem Mansoor. London: Routledge and Kegan Paul, 1973.

Idel, Moshe. *Kabbalah: New Perspectives*. New Haven: Yale University Press, 1988.

Jacobs, Andrew S. *Christ Circumcised: A Study in Early Christian History and Difference*. Philadelphia: University of Pennsylvania Press, 2012.

Jenkins, Richard. *Rethinking Ethnicity*. London: Sage, 2008.

Johnson, David W. "Further Remarks on the Arabic History of the Patriarchs of Alexandria." *Oriens Christianus* 61 (1977): 103–116.

Juasson, Antonin, and Rafaël Savignac. *Mission archéologique en Arabie*. Paris: E. Leroux, 1909–22.

Kearney, Richard. *The Wake of the Imagination: Ideas of Creativity in Western Culture*. London: Hutchinson, 1988.

Khan, M. ʿA. "Kitabu Taʾbi-ir-ruya of Abu ʿAli b. Sina." *Indo-Iranica* 9, no. 4 (1956): 43–77.

Kohlberg, Etan. "The Term 'Rāfida' in Imāmī Shīʿī Usage." *Journal of the American Oriental Society* 99, no. 4 (1979): 677–679.

Kugle, James L. *In Potiphar's House: The Interpretive Life of Biblical Texts*. Cambridge, MA: Harvard University Press, 1990.

Kuschel, Karl-Josef. *Abraham: Sign of Hope for Jews, Christians, and Muslims*. Translated by John Dowden. New York: Continuum, 1995.

Kushner, Tony, and Alisa Solomon, eds. *Wrestling With Zion: Progressive Jewish-American Responses to the Israeli-Palestinian Conflict*. New York: Grove Press, 2003.

Laqueur, Walter, and Barry Rubin, eds. *The Israel-Arab Reader: A Documentary History of the Middle East*. 7th rev ed. London and New York: Penguin, 2008.

Lassner, Jacob. "Genizah Studies in the United States: Its Past and Its Future Links to Near Eastern Historiography." In *A Mediterranean Society By S. D. Goitein: An Abridgement in One Volume*, edited by Jacob Lassner, 469–481. Berkeley: University of California Press, 1999.

Lecker, Michael. *The Constitution of Medina: Muḥammad's First Legal Document*. Princeton: Darwin Press, 2004.

Levy, Jakob. *Chaldäisches Wörterbuch über die Targumim und einen grossen Teil des rabbinischen Schriftthums*, 2 vols. Leipzig: Verlag von Baumgärtner's Buchhandlung, 1876–89.

Lewis, Bernard. "An Apocalyptic Vision of Islamic History." *Bulletin of the School of Oriental and African Studies* 13 (1950): 308–338.

———. *The Jews of Islam*. Princeton: Princeton University Press.

Lobel, Diana. *A Sufi-Jewish Dialogue: Philosophy and Mysticism in Baḥya Ibn Paquda's Duties of the Heart*. Philadelphia: University of Pennsylvania Press, 2007.

Lowney, Chris. *A Vanished World: Muslims, Christians, and Jews in Medieval Spain*. Oxford and New York: Oxford University Press, 2005.

Maimonides, David b. Joshua. *Al-Murshid ilā-l-tafarrud wa-l-murfid ilā-l-tagarrud*. Edited and translated into Hebrew by Paul B. Fenton. Jerusalem: Meqize Nirdamim, 1985.

Maimonides, Moses. *The Guide of the Perplexed*, 2 vols. Translated by Shlomo Pines. Chicago: University of Chicago Press, 1963.

Maimonides, Obadyāh. *The Treatise of the Pool*. Translated by P. Fenton. London: Octagon Press, 1981.

Mazuz, Haggai. *The Religious and Spiritual Life of the Jews of Medina*. Leiden: Brill, 2014.

Menocal, María Rosa. *The Ornament of the World: How Muslims, Jews, and Christians Created a Culture of Tolerance in Medieval Spain*. New York: Back Bay Books, 2002.

Morris, Benny. *Righteous Victims: A History of the Zionist–Arab Conflict, 1881–2001*. New York: Vintage, 2001.

Naveh, Joseph. "A Bilingual Burial Inscription From Saba." *Leshonenu* LXV, no. 2 (2003): 117–120.

———. "Seven New Epitaphs From Zoar." *Tarbiz* LXIX (1999–2000): 619–635.

Nebes, Norbert. "The Martyrs of Najrān and the End of Ḥimyar: On the Political History of South Arabia in the Early Sixth Century." In *The Qur'ān in Context: Historical and Literary Investigations Into the Qur'ānic Milieu*, edited by Angelika Neuwirth, Nicolai Sinai, and Michael Marx, 27–59. Leiden: Brill, 2010.

Neusner, Jacob, Tamara Sonn, and Jonathan E. Brockopp, eds. *Judaism and Islam in Practice: A Sourcebook*. London: Routledge, 2005.

Newby, Gordon D. *A History of the Jews of Arabia: From Ancient Times to Their Eclipse Under Early Islam*. Columbia: University of South Carolina Press, 1988.

———. "The Jews of Arabia at the Birth of Islam." In *A History of Jewish-Muslim Relations: From Their Origins to the Present Day*, edited by Abdelwahab Meddeb and Benjamin Stora, 39–51. Princeton: Princeton University Press, 2013.

———. *The Making of the Last Prophet: A Reconstruction of the Earliest Biography of Muhammad*. Columbia: University of South Carolina Press, 1989.

Oz, Amos. "For Its Survival, Israel Must Abandon the One-State Option." *Los Angeles Times*, March 7, 2015.

Pines, Shlomo. "Jewish Christians of the Early Centuries of Christianity According to a New Source." *Proceedings of the Israel Academy of Sciences and Humanities* 1, no. 13 (1966): 1–73.

———. "Maimonides' Halakhic Works and the *Guide of the Perplexed*." In *Maimonides and Philosophy*, edited by S. Pines and Y. Yovel. Dordrecht: Martinus Nijhoff, 1986.

———. "Shi'ite Terms and Conceptions in Judah Halevi's *Kuzari*." *Jerusalem Studies in Arabic and Islam* 2 (1980): 165–225.

Pourjavady, Reza, and Sabine Schmidtke. *A Jewish Philosopher of Baghdad: 'Izz al-Dawla Ibn Kammūna (d. 683/1284) and His Writings*. Leiden: Brill, 2009.

Pseudo-Dionysus of Tel-Mahre. *Chronicle II*. Edited by J. B. Chabot. Paris: CSCO, 1933. Translated by Witold Witakowski. Liverpool: Liverpool University Press, 1996.

Ravitzky, Aviezer. *Messianism, Zionism, and Jewish Religious Radicalism.* Translated by Michael Swirsky and Jonathan Chipman. Chicago: University of Chicago Press, 1996.

Robin, Christian. "Ḥimyar et Israël." *Comptes-Rendus de l'Académie des Inscriptions et Belles-Lettres* (2004): 831–908.

Rosenblatt, Samuel. *The High Ways to Perfection of Abraham Maimonides.* New York: Columbia University Press, 1927.

Schirmann, Hayyim. "The Life of Judah Halevi." *Tarbiz* 9 (1937–1939): 35–54, 219–240, 284–305; 10 (1938–1939): 237–239; 11 (1939–1940): 125.

Scholem, Gershom. *Sabbatai Sevi: The Mystical Messiah.* Translated by R. J. Zwi Werblowsky. Princeton: Princeton University Press, 1973.

———. "Sprouting of the Horn of the Son of David: A New Source From the Beginnings of the Doenme Sect in Salonica." In *In the Time of Harvest: Essays in Honor of Abba Hillel Silver*, edited by Daniel Jeremy Silver, 368–386. New York: Macmillan, 1963.

Shapira, Yitzack, and Yosef Elitzur. *Torat haMelekh.* Yeshivat Od Yosef Chai, N.P. 2009.

Shoemaker, Stephen J. *The Death of a Prophet: The End of Muhammad's Life and the Beginnings of Islam.* Philadelphia: University of Pennsylvania Press, 2012.

Skinner, Quentin. *The Foundations of Modern Political Thought.* Cambridge: Cambridge University Press, 1978.

———. "Meaning and Understanding in the History of Ideas." *History and Theory* 8 (1969): 3–53.

Smith, Jonathan Z. "What a Difference a Difference Makes." In *"To See Ourselves as Others See Us": Christians, Jews, and "Others" in Late Antiquity*, edited by Jacob Neusner and Ernest Frerichs, 3–49. Chico: Scholars Press, 1985.

Spencer, Robert, ed. *The Myth of Islamic Tolerance: How Islamic Law Treats Non-Muslims.* Amherst: Prometheus Books, 2005.

Steinschneider, Moritz. "Apocalypsen mit polemischer Tendenz." *Zeitschrift der Deutschen Morgenlandischen Gesellschaft* 28 (1874): 627–659.

Stetkevych, Jaroslav. *Muhammad and the Golden Bough: Reconstructing Arabian Myth.* Bloomington: Indiana University Press, 1996.

Stillman, Norman. *The Jews of Arab Lands: A History and a Sourcebook.* Philadelphia: Jewish Publication Society of America, 1979.

Stroumsa, Sarah. *Dāwūd Ibn Marwān al-Muqammiṣ's Twenty Chapters ('Ishrun al-Maqāla).* Leiden: Brill, 1989.

———. *Maimonides in His World: Portrait of a Mediterranean Thinker.* Princeton: Princeton University Press, 2009.

Tessler, Mark. *A History of the Israeli–Palestinian Conflict*, 2nd ed. Bloomington: Indiana University Press, 2009.

Tucker, William Frederick. *Mahdis and Millenarians: Shī'ite Extremists in Early Muslim Iraq.* Cambridge: Cambridge University Press, 2008.

Vajda, Georges. *L'Amour de Dieu dans la théologie juive du Moyen Âge*. Paris: J. Vrin, 1957.

———. *La Théologie ascétique de Baḥya ibn Paqūda*. Paris: Imprimerie Nationale, 1947.

Wasserstein, David J. "The Muslims and the Golden Age of Jews in al-Andalus." *Israel Oriental Studies* 17 (1997): 109–125.

Wasserstrom, Steven M. *Between Muslim and Jew: The Problem of Symbiosis Under Early Islam*. Princeton: Princeton University Press, 1995.

Watt, W. Montgomery. *Islamic Creeds: A Selection*. Edinburgh: Edinburgh University Press, 1994.

Wolfson, Elliot R. *Through a Speculum that Shines: Vision and Imagination in Medieval Jewish Mysticism*. Princeton: Princeton University Press, 1997.

Yeor, Bat. *The Dhimmi: Jews & Christians Under Islam*. Translated by David Maisel. Madison: Fairleigh Dickinson University Press, 1985.

Ziai, Hossein, and Ahmed Alwishah, eds. *Ibn Kammūna: Al-Tanqīḥāt fī sharḥ al-talwīḥāt. Refinement and Commentary on Suhrawardī's Intimations: A Thirteenth Century Text on Natural Philosophy and Psychology*. Costa Mesa: Mazda Publishers, 2003.

Index

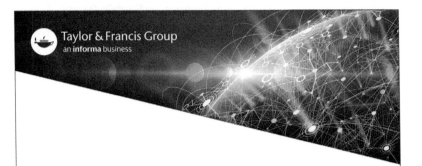

For Product Safety Concerns and Information please contact our EU representative GPSR@taylorandfrancis.com Taylor & Francis Verlag GmbH, Kaufingerstraße 24, 80331 München, Germany

Batch number: 08153772

Printed by Printforce, the Netherlands